RESTORING OLD HOUSES

RESTORING OLD HOUSES

NIGEL HUTCHINS

VNR

To Donna Hutchins

Published simultaneously in the United States of America by
Van Nostrand Reinhold Company, New York

Library of Congress Catalogue Number 80-50580

CANADIAN CATALOGUING IN PUBLICATION DATA
Hutchins, Nigel, 1945-
    Restoring old houses

ISBN 0-442-29625-8

1. Dwellings – Remodeling.   I. Title.
TH4816.H88   643´.7   C80-094623-5

EDITORIAL CONSULTANT: James T. Wills
DESIGN: Brant Cowie/Artplus Ltd.
PEN AND INK DRAWINGS: John Player
DIAGRAMS: Graham Thomas
FRONT JACKET PHOTOGRAPH: Paterson Photographic Works
BACK JACKET PHOTOGRAPH: Arthur Holbrook
TYPESETTING: Trigraph Inc.
FILM: Graphic Litho-Plate
PRINTING: McLaren, Morris and Todd Limited
BINDING: The Bryant Press Limited

Printed and Bound in Canada
80 81 82 83 84 85 86 7 6 5 4 3 2 1

ACKNOWLEDGMENTS

The author would like to thank those who allowed their
homes to be photographed, in particular the following
people: Mr. & Mrs. Jerry Ballantine, Mr. & Mrs. Berkley, Mr. &
Mrs. Jan Bos, George & Patricia Brinkerhoff, Bev Davis & Rick
Litchfield, Bob & Joan Day, Blair Drawson & Bibi Kaspari,
Mr. & Mrs. Ellis, Mrs. Fleming, Jeff, Liesl & Joshua Fuson, Guy
& Ellen Gelinas, Drs. Paul & Lorna Gendreau, Mr. &
Mrs. Hilton, Mr. & Mrs. Don Hobbs, David Honeywell, Dr. Jeff
& Ina Jackson, Tony & Sharon Jenkins, Air Vice Marshall Max
& Virginia Martyn, Blake & Ruth McKendry, Jim & Zilda Milne,
Mr. & Mrs. Alfie Miner, Mr. & Mrs. Bing Peart, Tim & Gerda
Potter, Paul & Paula Pringle, Dr. & Mrs. Robert Rae, Sandra S.
Rice, Major General & Mrs. R.P. Rothschild, Mel & Jean
Shakespeare, Mr. & Mrs. Bradbrooke Smith, Mr. & Mrs. Colin
Stephens, Mr. & Mrs. Rob Stuart, Sandra Todd, Donald & Lois
Tucker, Mr. & Mrs. B. Tyson. He would also like to thank The
Old House Journal, King's Landing and Upper Canada Village
for their assistance.

All photographs in the book are by Arthur Holbrook with
the exception of the following: Leo Berkowich, 15 (top right);
Nigel Hutchins, 16 (top), 29, 30 (right), 79 (bottom right), 87
(bottom), 98 (bottom), 131 (top center), 137 (top left), 138
(bottom left), 148 (bottom); Philip Jago, 32; Chris Reardon,
118; Robert Rothschild, 102 (center); Eleanor Sim, 55
(bottom); Craig Simms, 148 (top), 151 (bottom), 189; Wayne
Throop, 213; Tourist Branch, Province of Quebec, 91; Martin
Weaver, 35 (top), 34, 35 (bottom), 95, 171 (bottom right), 212;
Mark White, 15 (top left), 130, 139 (bottom left), 152 (bottom
left), 172 (left), 184 (right), 190 (right), 204.

Contents

Foreword   6

Preface   8

CHAPTER 1
The Philosophy of Preservation 10

CHAPTER 2
The Builders 24

CHAPTER 3
Lifestyles 38

CHAPTER 4
Research and Planning 52

CHAPTER 5
The Structure 72

CHAPTER 6
The Exterior 114

CHAPTER 7
Mechanical Systems 146

CHAPTER 8
Finishing 180

Appendix   217

Notes   221

Glossary   225

Bibliography   229

Index   234

Foreword

EARLY IN 1980 Nigel Hutchins came to see us at the Heritage Canada Foundation and we discussed his idea of producing a book to help the layman understand and practise the preservation of our architectural heritage. At first, it seemed to us that the subject was too broad to treat in anything but a superficial manner, a fault which occurs in many books on the subject. Happily, the installments that I received from the Hutchins' household near Merrickville, Ontario, indicated that the finished book, *Restoring Old Houses*, would not only fulfil the original outline but greatly assist both the novice and the experienced in approaching the old house.

For some time now one of my major concerns has been that there should be a steady increase in the quality and quantity of books available on the subject of architectural preservation. There is a great need for practical books in this field, and *Restoring Old Houses* is just such a work.

The preservation and recycling of older buildings to suit the uses of contemporary society can be economically viable. They are certainly desirable, because when properly handled they can prevent the almost criminal waste of resources and energy characteristic of the indiscriminate demolition of older buildings in recent decades.

Architectural preservation cannot be economically feasible or appropriate if it is carried out in a state of ignorance. An awareness of common problems and remedies, appropriate technologies, original methods of construction and decoration, and above all a knowledgeable, sympathetic attitude towards the past are essential to the success of the process. In the following pages, the author guides the reader through all the phases of preservation.

Here will be found an appropriate blend of fascinating, little-known historical facts and sound, down-to-earth practical information which are the result of Nigel Hutchins' many years of experience. In fact, *Restoring Old Houses* is itself a tool to assist you in the preservation and utilization of our architectural past.

Martin E. Weaver
DIRECTOR OF EDUCATION
AND TECHNICAL SERVICES,
HERITAGE CANADA FOUNDATION,
OTTAWA

Preface

ARCHITECTURE FOR EVERY MAN. Of what does it consist? What social events shaped its style? What climates governed its construction? The cultural mosaic that made up the settlement of North America left in its wake three hundred or so years of influences that are too diverse to analyze briefly. A continent of transplanted cultures has taken a long time to find a coherent tradition.

The highlights of this varied architectural tradition have already been well documented, preserved, and studied. But what of the lesser structures—the houses of the common people? Should the individual house of lesser style be unimportant in the social definition of an urban or rural community? What makes a community? Surely it is not only the finery but also the more humble.

The attitudes of the 1970s, and the social upheavals of that period, have spawned a renewed interest in the preservation of things past. The neighborhoods that were so despised and rejected in the mid-twentieth century have now been resurrected by a society searching for both tradition and practicality. These same ideals have resulted in a resurgence of interest in small town North America.

The residential landscape of three hundred years of settlement brings with it several problems: technical and aesthetic ones, but also problems of identity. Should we live in the past? Should the 1830 farmhouse be completely restored at all costs, or should we look for the mood and feel of the period? Just as styles and lifestyles affected generations past, we too must adapt.

The preservationist is not by definition a creator but one who preserves. Our imprint on the legacy of the past should harmonize the technology and lifestyles of today and the richness of the past. The guiding principle of the settlers — common sense — seems to lend itself to the preservationist's task. The pseudo-intellectual's theories do not stand up in practice, based as they are on semantics rather than on an honest evaluation of the structure. One wonders if these learned people will spend as much time in future, raving as eloquently as they do today about the past, when they come to examine twentieth-century subdivisions.

The trials and tribulations of the preservation process are many. To master the individual disciplines that made up the house might take a lifetime. This book must be viewed as a guide and a catalyst. I only wish I'd written it twelve years ago when I "knew everything."

I have been fortunate to be surrounded by people of talent, taste and patience, and I am grateful in particular to the following people: Daniel Lazosky, Jack McAdam, François Barbeau, Mr. and Mrs. Blake McKendry, Mr. and Mrs. M. Copeland, Mrs. W. Indewick, Mr. and Mrs. K. D. Lawless, Chris Porter, Mary Vaughn Herivault, Martin Weil, William Watson, Martin Weaver, Jacques Dailibard, Alfie Friedman, Glen Cunningham, John Wyatt, Howard Piersdorff, Gregory MacNamee, Grace Hensbee, Mr. and Mrs. L. J. Hutchins, Mr. and Mrs. S. Slivinski, Mark White, Craig Simms, Phillip Jago, Wayne Throop and David Koshman.

My associate and friend, Paul A. Croteau, has worked with me from the beginning. To him I am most grateful, because his talents and craftsmanship have brought my ideas to fruition. My family, who endured a legacy of fallen-down houses and at times a fanatical addiction to the subject, have stood by me with love, patience, and humor. To them I am eternally grateful. To my associates in this book, James T. Wills, Arthur Holbrook, Joan Bieman, Laurie Coulter, Graham Thomas and John Player, I am most thankful.

N. H.
MERRICKVILLE, ONTARIO
APRIL, 1980

CHAPTER ONE

The Philosophy of Preservation

© John Player '80

THE LURE OF THE PAST and the material trappings of bygone eras have implanted in each of us a quest for the security, real or imagined, that yesterday can give us. Observe the magic that is evoked by an old family portrait, by grandmother's flapper dress, or witness the seemingly insatiable appetite for the furniture our forefathers made and used. Nowhere is this fascination more evident than in the area in which we live – the home. Whether it be our ancestral home (an uncommon occurrence in our transient society) or the creation of a new family base, people have become aware of the joy that owning an older house can bring.

This is not a new phenomenon. The often outspoken nineteenth-century architect, A. J. Downing, in discussing the home in North America declared:

It would be a boon to the age, if some gifted artist would show the world the secret sources of the influence which Architecture wields in all civilized nations. This is as far beyond our province as our ability. Still, we must be indulged in a brief analysis of the elements of interest which Architecture possesses for the human mind, and a glance at the partially concealed sources of that power which it exerts over our hearts and understandings.

Something of this kind seems to us to be demanded by the inquiring mind and the expanding taste of our people; and Domestic Architecture itself, which, amid the louder claims of civil and ecclesiastical art, had been too much neglected, seems to demand a higher consideration in a country where the ease of obtaining a house and land, and the ability of almost every industrious citizen to build his own house, constitute a distinctive feature of national prosperity.[1]

Although individual abilities to own houses and land have changed somewhat since Downing's time, the "louder claims" that he speaks of are today primarily civil and appear in the form of rather faceless shopping centers, office buildings, and factories. To make way for urban sprawl and altered uses of the countryside, too often valuable older homes have been demolished. Out of the realization of this phenomenon has grown the idea that many of these older buildings should be preserved in some form or other.

As more and more people buy older homes, both in the largely Victorian and Edwardian cores of our cities and in the rural areas of our countryside, the process of revitalizing both the individual house and the surrounding neighborhood becomes not only a question of practical (economic and physical) needs, but also a philosophical statement of how the individual building or area should be treated.

The term *restoration* has all too often led the uninformed down the incorrect preservation path for the house in question and to needless expenditures.

The subject of architectural preservation (the area into which all restoration, recycling, etc. falls) can be broken down into specific sections which are a great aid in determining just how to approach a specific house.

Restoration is the process of accurately recovering the form and detail of a structure as it appeared at a particular period of time. This may include the demolition of later portions of the structure not in keeping with the period of restoration or replacing pieces of the original work. Frequently in the evolution of a building, changes improve the original structure. For example, a basic one-and-a-half storey rubble-stone cottage built around 1830 might be far more appealing and architecturally interesting in its 1845 version; that is, after the introduction of a dec-

This mid-nineteenth-century house
retains its early features and
charm.

orative bargeboard and porch or a center gable.

Restoration must capture not only the technical optimum of the period to which the house is being restored (including such things as saw cuts in planks and the correct nail types), but also the mood of that period.

Historical groups, governments, or the wealthy individual are best left to the exacting, financially draining, and quite often academically dry process of pure restoration.

Rehabilitation, on the other hand, is the process of returning a property to a state of utility, through repair or alteration. It makes efficient contemporary use of the building possible. Rehabilitation can be broken into two sections. The first is historical rehabilitation, the area in which many private individuals seem to feel most comfortable. The term may be defined as keeping the best period details of the house while allowing for the creature comforts and practicalities of twentieth-century living. In

Abandonment is frequently the fate of many of the structures that once formed the core of the urban scene. This derelict boarding house in Nova Scotia was built in the first quarter of the nineteenth century.

The formidable influence of the Victorian era is reflected in the form and stature of this restored town house.

This Second Empire house in Maine, built in the mid-nineteenth century, has always been maintained.

A new elegance and charm has been given to these somewhat plain, turn-of-the-century row houses in Toronto.

A hundred years of uninspired change made this log house a good subject for historical rehabilitation. Note the contemporary tin roof, a concession of historical accuracy to cost and long life-span.

This historical rehabilitation makes use of eighteenth-century Canadian furnishings to further enhance the mood of the period.

The eighteenth-century New England farmhouse, one of the classics of North American architecture.

The floor beams in this nineteenth-century room have been exposed to add an interesting design element to the room.

*A new house in the style of the
French Regime of Quebec.*

The classic one-and-a-half storey rubble-stone house of eastern Ontario, first quarter nineteenth century. Note the lack of a gable. Gables were often added to this style of house.

A one-and-a-half storey rubble-
stone house of the same period in
Lanark County, Ontario. To restore
this to an earlier period for the sake
of preservation would ruin the
charm and architectural excite-
ment of the later additions of gable, verandah, and decorative
bargeboard.

In the pure restoration, every detail must be exactly of the period. Upper Canada Village, Morrisburg, Ontario, first quarter nineteenth century.

ordinary usage, the term restoration often refers to historical rehabilitation.

The second section, adaptive rehabilitation, amounts to the use of the interior space in existing structures. Many older buildings have been sorely abused through climatic deterioration and human carelessness, with the result that only virtual shells are left. The preservationist, in this case, may have a form of reserved *carte blanche* to use the existing space as physical, mechanical, and financial needs deem practical. The best examples of this form of rehabilitation are usually found in the urban cores of our cities where large houses of earlier times were often divided into small apartments or made into rooming houses. The atmosphere of the period has been lost forever by landlords eager to squeeze every penny from each inch of space.

By its very nature adaptive rehabilitation is a compromise. It may be likened to a marriage of the old and new. Practically, financially, and aesthetically, it is the essence of the house reborn.

While in a discussion of preservation terminology with some restoration technology students, the noted restoration architect, Peter John Stokes, remarked: "One must always remember – in all facets of architectural preservation – the house is the master." Whether you are involved in restoration or rehabilitation, this must always be your guide.

As a related but separate issue, *reconstruction* is the process of reproducing, by new construction, the exact form and detail of an earlier structure. To re-create something of a bygone era is often an exercise in the pursuit of contemporary fashion, rather than a worthwhile statement of historic fact. For the academic, it can only hold the promise that with the passage of time it will become the real thing, along with the misconceptions and mistakes that were built in when it was constructed. For the layman, reconstruction is a costly luxury. Frequently, however, an earlier form may be combined with contemporary building methods, allowing the new structure to be put together economically while it retains the period form to which it is related.

CHAPTER TWO

The Builders

TO PRESERVE THE ARCHITECTURAL PAST, we must look to the past. Then, buildings were made by people, for people, and as they are today the builders were governed by various conditions. The Europeans that came to North America brought with them many preconceived ideas of what the house should consist, both in style and physical content. It should also be remembered that the social life of the vast majority of immigrants was contained within the family, and the house was the major physical expression of this fact.

During the late 1600s and early 1700s, settlements were fashioned after what had been left behind in Europe, with obvious concessions to the availability of materials. Early settlements of the English in Virginia and the French at Ile Saint Croix, Quebec, and Port Royal, Nova Scotia, attest to this observation. In 1702, Queen Anne ascended the throne of England and nearly a century of unprecedented English activity began. The next one hundred years were to dramatically carpet the English-speaking eastern United States and Canada not only with settlers but with adaptations of European architecture honed to the climate and economy of the new land.

Style and politics placed their stamp on New World architecture and so did the availability of materials and tools. In Europe, craftsmen (the joiner, the framer, and the blacksmith, for instance) abounded, but their presence in the first wave of settlement in the Americas was not exactly overwhelming. Not only were there few craftsmen, but all tools had to come from Europe. As late as 1820, in the primarily Scottish settlement of Lanark County, Ontario, the government issued:

To each group of four families . . . a grindstone and a cross-cut and whip-saw; each family received an adze, hand-saw, drawing knife, shell auger, two gimlets, door-lock and hinges, scythe and snath, rasping-hook, two hoes, hay fork, skillet and camp kettle, and a blanket for each member of the family.[1]

The new settlements often demanded of their inhabitants tediously long days. They had to build a house, and their tools, utensils, and furniture were also frequently made by their own hands. The actual farming of the land made up the bulk of the time.

In a few instances, houses were provided. The importance of religion in almost all communities led to the building of a new house for the pastor. As the importance of the various trades evolved, the community might build quarters for the craftsmen as well. For example, in Quebec during the 1600s, French landowners and religious orders brought their own craftsmen with them and provided for them as in the Continental system.

The primary concern of the settlers was to build a shanty or hovel for protection from the climate and, in most cases the Indians, as soon as possible. When times got a bit better, a more substantial structure was erected.

The early house builders in North America fell into two categories. The first was the trained craftsman, who would have been schooled as an apprentice from childhood. He would eventually become a master craftsman with his own apprentices and shops. Associations or guilds are well documented in the French Regime of Quebec:

There was an annual procession of the Blessed Sacrament, and each group of craftsmen would be preceded by a banner. The first procession in which the woodworkers are reported to have taken part was in 1648. Next came the Indians led by Father LeJeune who

was dressed in surplice and stole; there followed twelve torches carried by twelve craftsmen of different trades: turner, woodworker, cobbler, cooper, locksmith, armorer, carpenter, mason, toolmaker, baker, cartwright, and nailer. . . .[2]

The second category of builder (and probably the more numerous) was the homegrown, itinerant builder, who, armed with some talent, constructed the domestic architecture of North America.

By the third quarter of the eighteenth century, specialization began, resulting in the first wave of architect-builders. Both the schooled and the self-taught builder were influenced by three things: memory (tradition), architects (Sir Christopher Wren or the Adam brothers, for example), and architectural handbooks. The importance of these handbooks cannot be underestimated. Combined

The primeval forest provided building materials of immense proportions. This example is thought to
have been constructed by the military, early practitioners of the log-
building art.

A

B

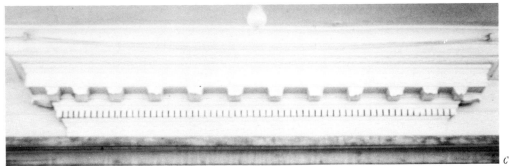

C

Architects of the past often designed not only the structure but also the furnishings. Notice the similarity of armoire(B) and porch(C) details in these eighteenth-century Quebec examples. A delightful climatic adaptation is visible in (A) and (D); the owner recounted that the snow was always so heavy that in 1840 his ancestors had to add a storm porch.

D

*An Adamesque mantel and fire-
board. Ontario, 1825-1835.*

*An Adamesque door surround.
Quebec, last quarter eighteenth century.*

with the adaptive skills of the North American builder, they formed the foundation of domestic architecture on this continent. This combination is well documented in the work and influence of Samuel McIntyre of Salem, Massachusetts. Although not a trained architect, McIntyre was greatly influenced by the Adam brothers, that *tour de force* of the Georgian period, who issued both design manuals and a type of catalogue of architectural components. McIntyre's work between 1782 and 1810 shows the results of this influence. His construction company was renowned for its house-building ability, and McIntyre himself personally designed and built many of the mantels and door surrounds for his houses. His shops trained apprentices and his Renaissance-like manner attracted disciples, who later went on to affect North American architecture in their own right. Batty Langley, Robert Morris, and

Asher Benjamin all operated in a similar manner, continuing the tradition begun with the 1714 publication of the English translation of Palladio's handbook.[3]

The first quarter of the nineteenth century was not an age of artistic enlightenment in North America. Politics, business, and exploration were still the dominant forces. Students of the "building" in North America might well be thankful for the

*The Crysler house, Upper Canada
Village, Morrisburg, Ontario,
1800-1810, a fine example of
Georgian architecture in the
Loyalist tradition.*

Family and religion were very important to the early pioneers. The influences of Georgian architectural style did not go unnoticed even in the churches and domestic buildings of rural Quebec.

Greek War of Independence in 1821, because the "newfound" birthplace of democracy stirred hearts, Loyalist and Republican both, that had not too long ago been involved in their own war of independence. The Greek Revival style that resulted abetted the rise of the master builder. In 1833, Minor Le Fave published *The Modern Builder's Guide* and, along with Asher Benjamin's *Practical House Carpenter* (1841), it became the bible of taste and construction.

The rawness and beauty of the wilderness seemed to lead these master builders to take the dryness out of traditional styles. The Georgian house, in particular, seemed to suit both the times and the climate; the pleasing proportions and balance of elements appealed to Canadians and Americans looking for order and respectability. The amount of light admitted by the large Georgian windows and the warming and cooling effects of the traditionally thick stone and brick facades adapted readily to the diverse climates of the east coast. European plans were often altered by the builder to suit local conditions and, as a result, widespread vernacular styles popped up and the builder's reputation grew.

One of the most delightful ways to visualize this movement is by visiting an old homestead. Often, one may see the remains of the original shanty, nearby is a log house, a bit further off is a modest but attractive stone or brick house, while separated by considerable space is the Victorian mansion.

The Victorian Period, although a time of rampant conservatism and propriety (table legs were often clad in skirts so as not to expose their naughty nakedness), also gave birth to what is one of the few truly American styles. The American Romanesque

The Gilroy Settlement, Lanark County, Ontario, circa 1850, a layout of convenience and harmony.

Revival is frequently called Richardson Romanesque. Henry Richardson (1876–1893) did much to lighten the oppressive Victorian Gothic style of the previous two decades. He was trained in France, and while the Civil War wracked the United States, he honed his craft in the office of the great French architect Labroust. Richardson's stay in France was enlightening, but he was plagued with depression over the war at home and personal financial problems. However, on returning to the United States he found himself in an enviable position. Most other architects were self-taught, but because of his formal training, married to his romantic vision of America and dedication to his work, Richardson was light-years ahead of the competition.

The present-day preservationist might well put Richardson's axioms into practice. He joined craftsmen, builders, architects, as well as artists, into one unified team – each element of their work a study in excellence. No competitive bidding ever took place on a Richardson project; quality was the goal. It is precisely this bidding that is so common today, with the result being over-expenditures and shoddy, uncaring work – the craftsmen driven only by the dollar.

Until the Industrial Revolution, all construction was done by hand. Hand tools, the ability to use them and the materials that were available were all important in this process. Wide pine planks, for example, were usually pit sawn by two men. The first stood above the pit taking one end of the saw, and the second stood below in the pit taking the other end. It is little wonder that we prize such planks today. Later, of course, planks were cut in water-powered sawmills, as were large structural members. Because of the relative ease of production in what we would consider primitive mills, the mill owner often became an important man in the community.

Even the nails used in construction were hand-wrought by the blacksmith. The earliest were "rose-headed" nails with the characteristic stamp of the smith's hammer on the head. As time passed, nail mills were erected. They turned out the

Stone-curved sawing, 1872.

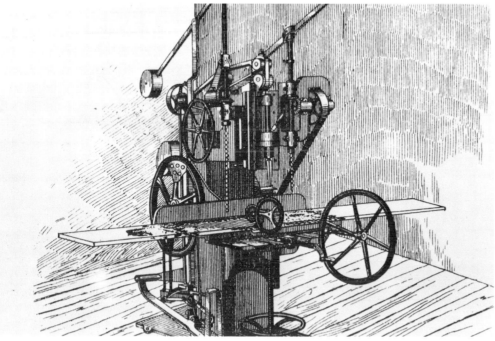

Boring and mortising machine, 1876.

The mass-produced house was a direct result of the technological innovations of the Industrial Revolution.

The terra cotta detailing on this Victorian row house was made in a beehive kiln, an innovation of the Industrial Revolution.

identifiable square or "cut" nails made by water-powered machines out of bars of iron nail stock. The blacksmith was also responsible for much of the interior hardware of the house, from the Norfolk latches on the doors to the all-important fireplace crane and cooking implements.

Once the Industrial Revolution came, there were major changes in construction methods, due to the easy availability of cut lumber, machine-made nails, and standardized glass. Hardware that was once laboriously wrought by the smith could now be quickly stamped out by steam-driven machines. Mouldings, originally hand-planed, were now created in seemingly endless lengths by complex machinery. The very character of the houses that resulted changed, for they too took on the mass-produced look of the post-revolution.

CHAPTER THREE

Lifestyles

TODAY, THE LIFESTYLE of the individual or family group governs the use of the space in which we live. This was no different in the past. To preserve an old house without understanding and interpreting the lifestyle of those who lived in the house before us is to ignore life itself. Whether in an urban or rural setting, the same questions we ask ourselves may be applied to the structure's early occupants. Were they rich or poor? Did they entertain? How did climate affect the way they lived?

In rural Ontario through the 1800s, for example, we not only find the buildings forming a pattern of harmony with the landscape, but also a pattern of convenience. The natural layout of the land and the farmer's demands on it gave rise to an unconscious form of estate planning. Observe the use of a summer kitchen to escape the heat of cooking in summer, the placement of the woodshed behind the summer kitchen, and the drive shed close to that. The barn was often placed beside a stream but situated just out of reach of the spring flood. These were common sense decisions in a climate where mistakes frequently threatened existence.

It was not uncommon to have the livestock share part of the house in winter, both for their survival and, one suspects, for that of their owners. In late seventeenth-century Boston, "the poultry had their breakfast usually in cold weather in the kitchen."[1] This kind of accommodation was necessary during weeks of bitter winds, snow, and ice when lean-tos or single-board-sided sheds offered scant protection. Ewes, young calves, piglets, and hens could be saved from freezing if they were moved into the shelter of the kitchen hearth.

Such care enabled hens, wakened by the light of flames seen through uncurtained windows, to save the lives of a Massachusetts family in December 1640:

Mr. Pelham's house in Cambridge took fire in the dead of the night by the chimney [and was] ready to lay hold upon the stairs. A neighbour's wife, hearing some noise among her hens, persuaded her husband to arise, which being very cold he was loth to do, yet through her great importunity he did and so espied the fire, and came running in his shirt, and had much to do to awake anybody, but he got them up at last and so saved all.[2]

In eastern Ontario, the James house on the Franktown Road in Lanark County is a prime example of a site where this manner of housing the animals was practised, and it is safe to assume that the custom was more widespread.

Settlement patterns in urban areas frequently followed similarly logical growth. River travel meant relatively dense settlement at a stopping-off point, for instance. As an area was opened, different trade routes, commercial centers, and the inevitable housing developed. Row housing was the result of limited space in these centers.

Early concerns for protection from the elements and ease of assembly eventually gave way to parlors and a more "civilized" way of life, although the kitchen still remained the heart of the house. Bread continued to be baked, either in built-in fireplace ovens or larger outdoor ovens.

The bedchamber was the first "new" room of the house; it was usually located on the ground floor where it could be heated to some extent. A family would be fortunate to have more than one bed, with perhaps a trundle bed underneath that could be

*Jonas Robinson of Leeds County,
Ontario, recently documented the
layout of his farm in this delightful
naïve painting.*

In this house, the stone kitchen leads to the summer kitchen, drive shed, and woodshed; a pattern of convenience.

rolled out at night. It was quite normal for mother, father, and all the children up to their teenage years to sleep in one area. Inventories of early dwellings indicate that bed furniture such as hangings or curtains was relatively uncommon, while ticks and shakes were numerous, sleeping on the floor being the result.[3]

Initially, the bedroom would be a partitioned area of the main room, and later an upstairs area as we now know it was constructed. Throughout eastern North America, the upper storey was only used during spring, summer, and fall. Even in major houses, it was not unusual to sleep downstairs in winter beside the stove, the upstairs having been sealed off against the cold.

As conditions improved, civility quickly spread into the established urban centers, and city houses were built complete with parlors and dining rooms.

Since most rural settlement patterns followed major rivers and their tributaries, the improvement in transportation systems soon caused these more elegant rooms to be found in most rural communities as well.

In *At Home in Upper Canada*, Jeanne Minhinnick points out that

the parlour was a significant room for families who had been confined to kitchen and bedrooms for a long time. People were at home a great deal more than they are today and spent much time together as a family. Even in houses which had been divided to afford separate quarters for the elderly, or for a young married son and his family, the parlour in warm weather was generally the common sitting room.[4]

The parlor was a place of family pride, where all the best furniture was displayed. Unlike other parts of the house, it may even have had window curtains.

James house, Lanark County, Ontario, circa 1825. The left side of the house was used as a barn for the animals.

Outside bake house. Eastern Ontario, first quarter nineteenth century.

The Indian shutter was a sliding shutter, reputedly used for protection against Indian arrows. Maine, last quarter eighteenth century.

As the Industrial Revolution ate up valuable land for industry, the Victorian row house represented both a new affluence and a judicious use of limited space.

Its construction included the selection of knot-free planks for the floors and the addition of a cornice and chair-rail. More ambitious examples would have had built-in cupboards to show off the best china.

When restoring or rehabilitating an early house these living patterns should be kept in mind. Furnishing, too, is the oft forgotten element of architec-tural preservation.[5] "There are no cupboards," the would-be preservationist cries unknowingly, over-looking the armoires, Welsh dressers, and pie cup-boards that held our forefathers' trappings. These, of course, have long since been removed. Unfor-tunately, built-in cupboards are frequently intro-duced into rooms originally meant only to hold a bed and a small candlestand. The congestion caused

Period colors and furnishings in
this restoration express the mood of
of the nineteenth century.

by the new cupboard results in even less storage area, defeating the exercise altogether.

The kitchen, where today we clamor for built-in cupboards and counters, was primarily a work area with a table for preparation, some open shelving and, more often than not, an open dresser to store china and cutlery. Herbs were hung from a rack above the fire, while many of the actual cooking utensils surrounded the fireplace. Until the turn of the century, every home had some space for food storage, either in the form of a root cellar or a pantry extension of the kitchen. Today, these areas have been replaced by the freezer.

To impose one's own family lifestyle on another's dwelling requires much soul-searching and compromise. The settler constructed a custom-built

Simplicity of line and form in a rehabilitated early twentieth-century house.

This built-in cupboard and Dutch armoire work as effectively today as they did 150 years ago.

What better way to store dishes in the period kitchen.

*Contemporary furnishings accent
the stark redesign of the interior of
this house, which was built in the
1930s.*

house based on the climate of the area and the social and economic needs of the family. The new tenant (for that is what all owners are in the history of a house) must adapt the structure to the requirements of his or her family. Even after two hundred years, these requirements are basically the same ones that the settler followed. The new tenant must study and respect what has gone before, not an

impossible task since the desire for an old house was obviously built on a love for the past. The new owner must leave the mark of that earlier lifestyle and period intact, while sympathetically and harmoniously meshing his own family's impact with that mark. Together they should present an important legacy for the generations to come.

*A mid-nineteenth-century kitchen
in a historical rehabilitation
utilizes period work and storage
areas as well as contemporary con-
veniences.*

Built-in modular kitchen units are compatible with a rehabilitation involving the use of available space.

CHAPTER FOUR

Research and Planning

TO BE A PLACE OF PRACTICALITY, function, form, humor, and sensibility the period house must echo its owner's wants and desires. Many things govern the architectural preservation process. A systematic approach must be taken at the outset to insure that all facets of the project are weighed carefully and assembled into one package that does justice both to the structure and the owner's needs.

To embark on this process, an initial investigation or analysis must take place. In the chart below, the house is broken into segments or architectural elements. They are examined and documented for period detailing and present condition, and obvious changes are noted, such as aluminum windows over six-over-six originals. This initial survey is done in order to give the new owner an accurate picture of the house in question. After this point it is usually possible to determine which preservation method to follow: historic or adaptive rehabilitation. By all rights, such an analysis should have been done prior to purchasing the property. Preconceived ideas and initial enthusiasm are quite severely dampened as a dissection uncovers many of the minor problems so casually breezed over by the realtor or previous owner.

Beside each of the entries in the chart you should note the present condition, the work needed and historical accuracy.

ANALYSIS OF STRUCTURE

SOCIAL PERIOD:
PHYSICAL PERIOD:
CONDITION TO PERIOD:
LOCATION:

ROOF:
Cladding (shingles, tin, etc.):
Flashing (chimneys, valleys):
Rafter Ends:
Soffit and Fascia:
Planking of Roof:
Eavestrough:
Bargeboard
Chimney (materials, pointing, etc.):

EXTERIOR:
Cladding:
Log:
Clapboard:

Board and Batten:
Joints (board and batten):
Deterioration: insect
                    rot
                    human abuse
Stone: decay (air pollution):
       moisture:
       human abuse:
       structural defects:
       pointing (quality of):
       replacement materials:

INTERIOR:
Structure:
Walls (plaster, lath):
Moulding (door trim,
          paneling, baseboard):
Doors:

Hardware:
Plasterwork:
Paint:
Stairs:
Railings:
Fireplaces:

INTERIOR (MECHANICAL):
Electrical:
Plumbing:
Heating:
Venting Systems:

STRUCTURAL FOUNDATION SYSTEM:

SITE ANALYSIS:
Levels:
Vegetation:
Drainage:

The burnt-out shell of this house (circa 1835) was carefully rehabilitated with great attention to period detail and form.

This is a perfect opportunity for historical rehabilitation because most of the period details are intact. Ontario, first quarter nineteenth century.

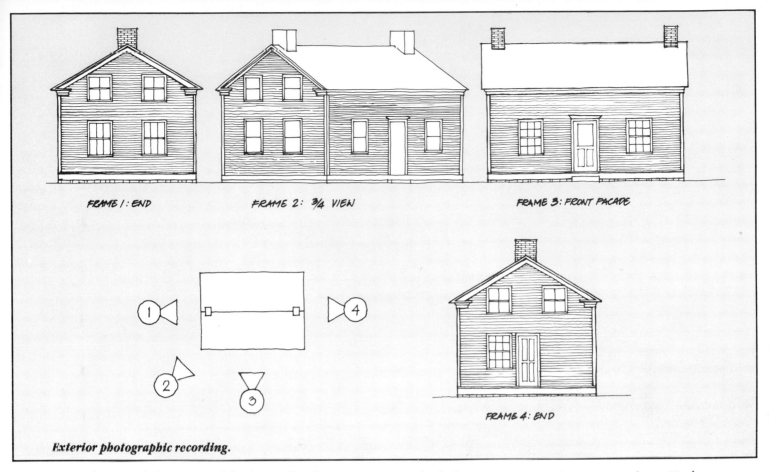

FRAME 1: END   FRAME 2: 3/4 VIEW   FRAME 3: FRONT FACADE

FRAME 4: END

Exterior photographic recording.

Once the initial diagnosis of the house has been completed, the decision of preservation methodology must be made. If a considerable portion of the house is in a preservable state to the period desired (say ninety per cent) and changes, such as additions and omissions, can be easily recognized and rectified, then historical rehabilitation should take place. Where major elements have been totally eliminated, it is better to compromise and utilize the area as living space to be designed around the remaining details than to guess at the early appearance of the house.

Up to this stage of the project, a restoration specialist may not have been called in, although the consultation of a professional during the structural analysis would be money well spent.

The three approaches to the actual process are the time plan, the self-contractor method, and one in which the entire project is contracted out. Each approach has distinct advantages and disadvantages. In the time plan, the work is spread out over one to five years and a set amount is accomplished each year. The advantages of this method include the fact that you will have longer to study the house and your lifestyle will evolve as the house evolves. As well, you will be able to pay as you go with relatively little pressure and a consequent enjoyment of the process. Specific jobs, such as drywall, wiring, and plumbing, can be completed at your own pace or contracted out as you need them. Long-term frustration, however, is one of the very real disadvantages of this approach, because living in a house while it is under construction can shake the strongest relationship. The cost of materials does not appear to be going down in the foreseeable future, so it is quite probable that you will be facing cost over-runs during the life of a time plan project. Health dangers (see page 74), fire hazards, and insurance problems all accompany this method. In fact, insurance rates may be incredibly high or coverage may not be available at all. In Canada, you will have to pay Workmen's Compensation. Time wasted and a general lack of time are two more drawbacks.

If you become a self-contractor, the time frame of the project is immediate, because you control the pace of the work. Advantages include the elimination of ten to twenty per cent contract fees, a complete and personal awareness of the house and its problems, as well as the satisfaction of having structured your own project. Being a self-contractor is time-consuming, though, and you will have to be on the site ninety per cent of the time to know what is happening. Other disadvantages are that you probably lack technical expertise, you will lose time due to improper scheduling of work, and you lack experience in finding good tradesmen. Both Workmen's Compensation (in Canada) and site insurance will have to be paid.

The time frame is also immediate when you contract out the entire project. On the plus side, you are dealing with set costs, "expert" workmanship, guarantees, and the fact that you will be able to move in once work is completed. This is the expensive approach. Also on the minus side is the tendency to miss research clues due to a lack of time during construction or an unwillingness to change once work has begun.

After you have chosen a plan and before actual work is started, ask yourself the following questions. Why did we buy an old house? Is everyone we talk to an expert? (Everyone seems to be an expert on the subject of old houses: architects, tradesmen, your best friend. All seem to have an intimate knowledge of your house and what is best for it.) Must everything be square and true? Must it all look new?

From the very beginning of the project, a log, both written and photographic, should be kept. As the house evolves, keeping track of where things were and how they fit together is imperative.

Photographs are an instant, accurate, cheap record of the subject. Detailed drawings, although necessary as the process goes on, are never enough on their own. Using them with photos gives a graphically clear picture.

For a photographic record, the building should be divided into five segments. Take *exterior general views*, including front, back, side, and roof. Record *exterior details*, such as stone, clapboard, windows, and doors. Photograph the *exterior landscape*, including the relationship of the house to the physical lay of the land. In urban settings, the relationship between the house and the entire streetscape is important. (Remember that rear and service entrances are frequently used more than the front door.) In rural areas, the relationship of the house to vegetation may be more significant. (Orange lilies and lilacs, for example, are classical markers of a rural nineteenth-century Ontario landscape.) Take a series of *interior general views*. Finally, record *interior details*, especially unusual elements, such as murals, decorative art, or stained glass. Also photograph period mechanical systems, such as gas lighting and heating apparatus.

When photographing the house, put some form of scale (a ruler or penknife, for example) into each frame to give you a sense of proportion. Remember that trees or furniture may mask important details

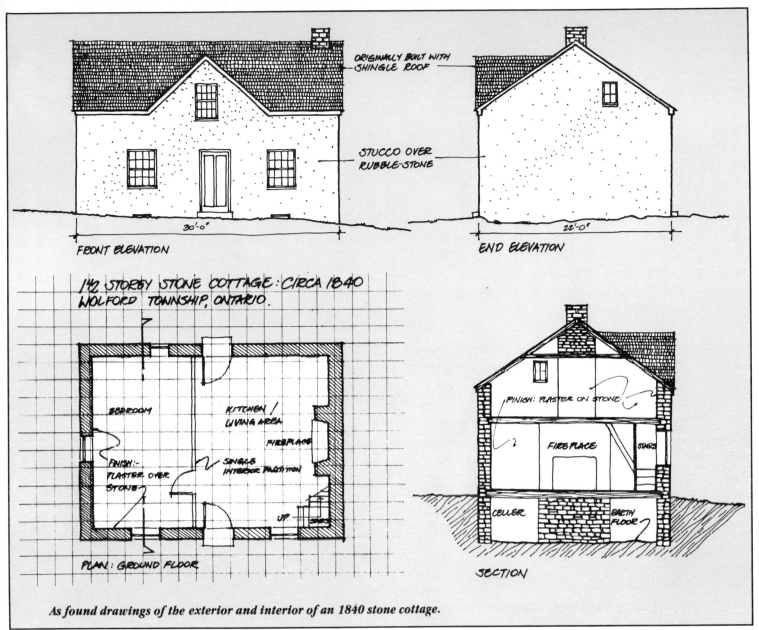

Labels within the illustration:

ORIGINALLY BUILT WITH SHINGLE ROOF

STUCCO OVER RUBBLE-STONE

FRONT ELEVATION

30'-0"

END ELEVATION

22'-0"

1½ STOREY STONE COTTAGE: CIRCA 1840 WOLFORD TOWNSHIP, ONTARIO.

BEDROOM

KITCHEN / LIVING AREA

FIREPLACE

FINISH:- PLASTER OVER STONE

SINGLE INTERIOR PARTITION

UP STAIRS

PLAN: GROUND FLOOR

FINISH: PLASTER ON STONE

FIRE PLACE

STAIRS

CELLER

EARTH FLOOR

SECTION

As found drawings of the exterior and interior of an 1840 stone cottage.

and more than one frame may be required to record a certain area. Obviously, if an architectural corner cupboard was an integral part of a room, to remove it would give a wrong impression of that area. Even bland, uninteresting rooms must be recorded both in general and in detail. Along with the more decorative areas of the house, an overall picture cannot be assembled without photographs of all the pieces.

Before starting your photo recording, it is wise to compile a simple sheet listing roll and negative number, subject, location, camera position, and date. In my own work, I use both black and white prints and color slides.

At the same time that photographic recording is taking place, a set of as-found drawings should be made. These are based on the present layout of the house: interior and exterior, locations of windows,

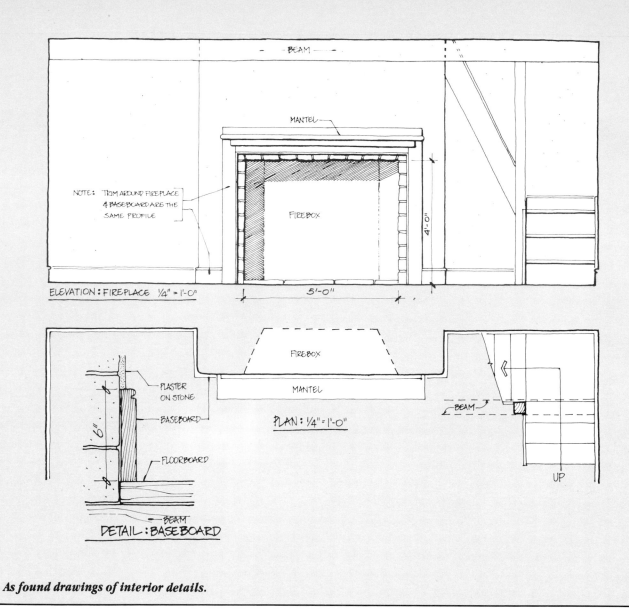

As found drawings of interior details.

doors, porches. Obvious problem areas in the structure should be noted on these plans, such as cracks in the foundation or loose plaster. Descriptions of each room should accompany the drawings, including the materials used in the room and approximate dating.

A grid should be laid out on paper and the house laid out on that grid; exterior elevations and dimensions, and then interior floor plans should be drawn. It is important to do this accurately, because it will form the plan from which any new design is taken.

RESEARCH

Historical and architectural research should be undertaken before imposing any form of change on the existing structure. Several basic but important questions need to be answered. Who built the house – a farmer, a craftsman, an architect? What is its date? What is its original style? What were the dates of major changes? What were the social strata of the builder and previous tenants? It is assumed that the legal description of the property has already been acquired.

There are three ways to obtain these answers and carry out your research. The first is to consult oral history, the second is to look at the physical evidence, and the third is to explore documentary sources.

The oral history of the house can be obtained by talking to the neighbors, the local merchants, or the postmaster. Rural areas are especially good for this, although folk legend and misconceptions often blur the facts. In Canada, one hundred to one hundred and fifty years of settlement is not a long time. Many older residents of an area may have been born in the late 1800s or the early 1900s and can recall their childhood surroundings well, surroundings that would not have changed much since initial settlement.

While doing the structural analysis, physical evidence may present itself through previously unnoticed details. Changes in moulding styles, framing techniques, and types of fastenings can all assist in answering your questions. Look at the structure as a giant jigsaw puzzle made up of many segments. Each segment may be broken into smaller sections, and so on. Look at each section independently, analyze it, see how it fits together.

When was it, for instance, that pit-sawn lumber stopped being used in your locale? Are the nails hand-wrought, hand and machine, or purely machine-made? What kind of screws, if any, are used? Styles of moulding and their panel design, different types of hardware – all give clues to the age of the house and periods of change.

The internal superstructure of the house quite often cannot be examined, although when it is possible, building techniques are often easy to date.

It is impossible to forget all preconceived notions of period, style and so on when researching. Let the evidence fall where it may in order to portray an accurate history of the house. The process of dating a building by style or any historical construction detail can lead to mistaken assumptions. A house with all the features of Georgian style in New England may be accurately dated 1770, but in areas of later settlement, such as the Niagara Peninsula in Ontario, a nearly identical structure may have been built in 1820. Early styles and construction methods survived primarily in rural areas where fashion or industrial development arrived years after its urban peak, and they were frequently based on the traditions current in the settlers' country of origin. Five to twenty years might have passed before an individual would copy a particular style in the New World.

Also remember that recycling is not a new fad. Just as today's preservationist scours the countryside for architectural elements (doors, mouldings, hardware) from less fortunate buildings, so too did the nineteenth-century builder. One six-panel door in Burritt's Rapids, Ontario, started life in the White Swan Hotel, moved next door to the miller's house, and was moved again to a timber-frame house across the road. Fortunately, all the houses shared the same period; the tell-tale paint trim, abbreviations in door size, and positioning of hardware enabled accurate identification.

FRENCH REGIME: BEFORE 1759, A TYPICAL 1½ STOREY STONE HOUSE OF THE
PERIOD, NOTE TRIPLE CHIMNEYS & DORMER WINDOWS. FIRST
STOREY WINDOWS WERE MULTIPANED CASEMENT

GEORGIAN TRADITION: FOLLOWING A BUILDING TRADITION STARTED UNDER
C. 1810   THE BRITISH KINGS OF THE PERIOD, THESE SOLID
2½ STOREY HOUSES BECAME POPULAR, WITH
BALANCED 3-5-7 BAY FACADES & CENTER DOORS.
HIP ROOF IS TYPICAL

NEO-CLASSIC: IN THE STYLE OF THE ADAM BROTHERS OF MID 18TH CENTURY
C. 1820   ENGLAND, THIS LOW-PITCHED GABLE ROOFED & 2½ STOREY
HOUSE HAS BALANCED FACADE - CENTER DOOR WITH FAN
TRANSOM, SIDE LIGHTS & CLASSICAL PEDIMENT &
COLUMNS

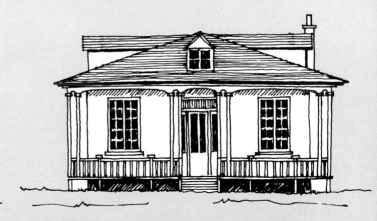

REGENCY: THIS 1½ STOREY HOUSE WITH GALLERY, LARGE
1810-40   WINDOWS & HIP ROOF ORIGINATES IN THE STYLE
TYPICAL OF 1811-1820 DURING GEORGE IV's
OFFICE AS BRITISH REGENT/PRINCE OF WALES

Domestic architectural styles.

CLASSIC REVIVAL: AN ADAPTION OF GREEK CLASSICAL TEMPLE-ELEGANT
C 1845   URBANE STRUCTURES WITH FLAT OR PEDIMENTAL
HOODS OVER WINDOWS & OPEN PORCHES SUP-
PORTED ON COLUMNS

PICTURESQUE: OFTEN QUITE SMALL, THESE HOUSES REFLECTED
C 1860   BUILDERS' OR OWNERS' INDIVIDUAL INTERPRETATION
OF THE GOTHIC REVIVAL

ITALIANATE: POPULAR AROUND THE TIME OF CONFEDERATION, THESE
C 1860   TOWN HOUSES OFTEN INCORPORATED A SQUARE
TOWER, EITHER CENTRAL OR ASYMMETRICALLY
LOCATED

SECOND EMPIRE: THE PROMINENT FEATURE OF THIS STYLE
C 1870   IS THE MANSARD ROOF, SEEN HERE WITH
A CONCAVE SLOPE

Machine-made lath in the kitchen indicates an early (circa 1890) alteration; the wainscot is original.

In dating the period house, pay attention to telltale elements like door hardware, construction methods, architectural style, recorded information, types of lath, wallpaper, and paint. Comparing the house in question to similar houses with known dates can often help determine when construction first began and when subsequent changes were made. These photographs are all from a Frankville, Ontario, farmhouse.

The original twelve-over-twelve windows were moved from the parlor to a nearby chicken house. The window style indicates a probable date in the mid-nineteenth century for original construction.

Original accordion lath and plaster with traces of horsehair are again characteristic of the 1830 period in this part of Ontario. The wallpaper dates from 1850-1860 and was probably imported from England or the United States.

A six-panel door with its Carpenter lock. Both are characteristic of the 1830 period in this area and narrow the dating process still further.

The pencil note on the siding reads, "310 greenwood, 52 seed, 130 lbs, pioneer large size, 1926." This is not directly related to architecture, but it does identify the farming life of a past tenant.

That a wall was moved at some earlier period can often be ascertained by lifting linoleum or later floors. The appearance of different periods or styles should neither alarm nor throw us off. Our ancestors renovated, just as we do today. As mentioned in Chapter 2, the earliest house was frequently merely one room. Rather than tear it down, a new house might have been built around it, using the original as a wing.

The genealogy of one house may serve as a good example of the changes and additions that an old house undergoes over time. In 1820, one Ontario house was a one-room shanty. By 1825, it had been expanded into a one-and-a-half storey rubble-stone cottage, with a built-in cupboard and several windows; it was heated by fireplace. A larger structure was built between 1830 and 1835, and the original structure served as a summer kitchen. The rooms

The present owner of this 1840s house is fortunate that changes made over the years were documented. The first photograph was taken circa 1865-1870 and shows the original form with early Victorian embellishment. In the second photograph, taken about 1890, a third storey and a tower have been added. The last view shows the house in its present condition.

were partitioned, partially because of stove heat. (At this stage and date in many houses, a gable appeared in front which became more severe in pitch as the Victorian era approached.) Ornate plasterwork, the highest degree of decor, was added around 1875, and in 1920 renovations took the form of tongue-and-groove paneling and tin ceilings.

An archaeological dig is the ultimate *in situ* research for physical evidence. Early foundations, travel patterns, garbage dumps all reveal a wealth of knowledge from the past. For the amateur in a rural situation, information and fun comes from a dig in the farm dump, which is usually easy to find even after one hundred years. A seemingly out-of-place mound or hillock, relatively close to the house, will frequently tell a tale. Two dumps ordinarily existed,

one summer and one winter, because travel through deep snow with a load of garbage was not a pleasant thought. One must remember to always approach a dig with sensitivity and caution; time and care must be allowed.

The gathering of documentary evidence from published or verbal sources is a slow process. A precise, systematic set of notes must be kept. Each entry should include the location of the document, the date when the notes were made, and whether the material inspected was an original or on microfilm. You should also record the name of the document, the volume number, the dates that it covers and the page numbers from which you have gathered your information. This may seem like a lot of work, but if your research spans several years of more or less sporadic investigation, it is easy to lose track of the origin of your notes.

If you haven't already done it, the legal description of the house may be easily found by looking at the tax bill. A trip to the local library is next. County directories (historic atlases in Ontario) are the first place to look; they can give enormous amounts of information, but caution should be exercised because they are not always accurate. Individuals paid to have their houses illustrated in these directories, and many an artist's imagination improved the overall appearance and landscape of the house. The premise here was that if the house looked good in the book, the artist would be rehired next year.

Cities often had yearly directories which listed the name of the householder (identified as the owner when necessary), the householder's occupation, and the number of boarders. This is a good way to find out about the tenants of the house; to find the social make-up of the neighborhood check other residents' occupations. All you need is an address in order to check a city directory.

In 1875, the Charles E. Goad Company commenced business in Canada; fire insurance maps and plans were their trade. Drawn to scale, these documents record industrial, commercial and, in early cases, residential buildings in fair detail. New buildings, schools, fires, and demolitions were included as each new issue came out. The Insurers' Advisory Organization (formerly the Canadian Underwriters' Association) bought the Goad Company. Today, at their head office in Toronto, period fire maps for eleven hundred Ontario communities are filed. Each province has a head office where maps for that province are kept and can be seen by appointment.

Past tax assessment rolls can be found at the town hall or county registry office. Pertinent information includes: the dimension of the property, the head of the household, his or her age, size of family, and religious persuasion. Registry offices will also provide: deeds, mortgage information, wills involving the property in question, court claims against the property, disputes about the property, and previous sale prices.

Lastly, but perhaps most satisfying, is the discovery of your property in an early sketch, painting, print, or photograph. Not only do you obtain a visual portrayal of the house, but also a clear picture of landscape, costuming of the inhabitants, and traffic patterns. All are guides to the activities and appearances of earlier times.

Where particular details are lost or in doubt, the preservationist must be able to let accumulated research serve as a guide for educated guesswork.

Explore your area for like details of the period in question. The mood and feel of a period is made up of many architectural ideals and elements. Your research should allow you to exercise your taste and sensitivity in using the styles that are in keeping with your house. For example, incorporating an oriel window in an 1820 Georgian house where before there was a blank wall enclosing a dark room is using your knowledge to advantage. You are, in fact, stealing a detail from your house's period that you know to be accurate in order to have a more pleasant room.

The kind of research outlined here must be done. There are no shortcuts. To ignore the past is to negate your reasons for acquiring an old house in the first place.

INTENDED LIFESTYLE

The evidence of your research has provided you with background on early living patterns, occupations of early tenants, and the shape and feeling of the period, while a structural analysis has shown what the house requires to put it into a reasonably accurate condition. At this point, the requirements of your intended lifestyle must be meshed with what you have learned. Quite often many changes that were originally thought necessary to accommodate a twentieth-century lifestyle can be freely omitted once the legacy of past families is known. It is unwise to think of cost at this time. To impose restrictions now will only hamper the preservation process; all too soon it will be affected when the dollar rears its lustful head.

Compile the following lifestyle chart and be honest with yourself in your answers.

Is this a permanent or summer home?
Will you live in it right away?
Is it a part-time hobby?

Social demands:
Do you both work?
Type of occupations?
How much free time?

Children:
What age(s)?
Are schools close (rural areas)?
Are friends close (rural areas)?
School bus?
Is a play area needed?

Long-range objectives:
Is it a permanent home (retirement)?
Do you intend to sell (perhaps for profit)?

Occupational center:
Is it your studio, office?
Work area?
Farm?
Do you need secretarial space?

Preferences:
Are you immaculately groomed, wear Gucci shoes
and drive a Mercedes?

Do you wear tweeds or blue jeans, have mud on
your boots and drive a Volvo?
Do you buy your clothes at Sears and drive a Chev?

Furnishings:
What furniture do you have?
What amounts of space are needed?
Do you collect antiques?
Will you sell your present furniture and begin col-
lecting?

Animals:
Dogs and cats, where will they eat and sleep?
In urban areas, where can they be walked?
Farm animals?

Hobbies:
Will the house be a hobby?
Outdoor sports?
Do you prefer films, museums, galleries, country
auctions?
Will you entertain a lot? If so, where?

Transportation:
Do you rely on public transit?
Do you have one or two cars?

Once you have answered these questions and
weighed their relative importance, considered the
requirements of the structural analysis, and digested
the results of your research, it is time to initiate the
formal planning stage.

FORMAL PLANNING: THE PERSONALITIES AND COSTS OF PRESERVATION

First of all, remember that a document or contract must be undertaken with everyone. All individuals must show samples of their work; references inspire confidence. You are the client, and as such you have the right to insist on the fulfillment of contract commitments. The duties of a restoration architect or designer include a structural analysis, the preparation of accurate estimates, a set of working drawings, and the actual running of the job. He or she will have a knowledge of historic building practices in your area and be able to design according to your needs and house. Such a professional will also have the experience to comply with contemporary building standards and codes, know the tradesmen who do the best work, and may be aware of funding sources that are open to you. Of course, a professional will have ready access to good sources of reproduction building materials. Ordinarily, the restoration architect will work either on an hourly rate or a percentage of the job. Some money down is a welcome gesture of intent on your part.

It is quite possible that an architect may wish to call in an engineer at some point, especially at the structural analysis stage. If you are reworking the house yourself, it is a good idea to have an engineer check your plans. He will be particularly important if you are analyzing period framing techniques.

In order to find first-class individuals, whether restoration architects, engineers, or tradesmen, you can consult schools of architecture, historical associations, and provincial or state preservation groups. It has been an unstated policy of most organizations not to specifically recommend individuals or companies for obvious reasons. Find a few in your area and look at their work, talk to their clients and choose. Everyone involved will have preconceived ideas of what an "old house" should look like; be forewarned.

An architect-designer must be an interpreter willing to compromise. He must be able to suppress his twentieth-century architectural self-image as visionary-artist-creator. That's already been done.

Find an architect-designer and a builder who are compatible, not only with each other, but also with you. You will spend lots of time with them and, after all, you are trusting them with your thoughts and money on probably the largest investment of your life. Be sure to tell them how much the house cost. Let them know what the budget is. Say who is in charge (husband, wife, dog). Be honest.

A lawyer is a necesary part of the team. He or she will provide general legal counsel, help you with information about the tricks of the building business, and assist you with such things as mechanics' liens. All parties need a legal document before any work should be allowed to commence. In my own work, the contract used outlines: the general terms of the job, the specific demands of the project, the cost, space for extras or work changes (until certain initial demolition has taken place, the amount of work required will often be uncertain), a time frame. I recommend that any changes or additions be dated, signed and witnessed. Both the client and his or her lawyer should read the contract carefully. This protects us (we have specified what we will do) and the client (if we do not do it).

FINANCING AND COSTS

Financing the rehabilitation of your old house is the final decision-maker in the process. Up to now, few financial restrictions have been placed on the investigation or plans for the house. Before making any decisions, you should consider this series of questions. How much was the property? How much have you got in hand? How much are you willing to borrow? How much is the house worth when you are finished, or, to be perfectly crass, what is the marketability of your home? The architect or the builder have the responsibility to let you know the value of similar houses in the area. These are real and often painful questions to answer, but the point is that they must be answered.

If you are seeking financial assistance for the project through a bank, credit union, or grant-giving institution, be prepared to submit specifications, a time schedule, drawings, insurance information, a list of the parties involved, and appraisals both before and after the work is completed.

CHAPTER FIVE

The Structure

THE BASIC CONDITION ANALYSIS described in Chapter 4 has no doubt revealed the odd crack in the wall, a small pond in the basement or perhaps a trampoline-like bounce in the living room floor. A house of any age will have some warps, bulges, and cracks. This is especially true of the period structure, but it is important to distinguish between blemishes due to age and more recent defects due to physical decay. This chapter deals with how to recognize real structural problems, trace their causes and take remedial action in the various areas and types of construction that the preservationist is likely to encounter.

Before beginning any work yourself, try to anticipate possible safety hazards. Think ahead and wear proper clothing for the job at hand. For any structural work, a hard hat is necessary, while strong work boots should always be worn. Using gloves during demolition seems obvious enough, but they are also a good idea when stripping paint.

Dust and fumes are major health considerations. Bird droppings, animal nests and some types of rot may contain toxic elements. Always vent the work area and wear a mask. Reasonably priced fabric masks are available at your local hardware store. Floor sanding, in particular, can be dangerous if lead-based paints are being removed. Paint removers give off toxic fumes, which have been known to cause heart attacks. Do not smoke when using a stripper, protect your eyes from splashes, and remember that gloves will protect hands from both chemicals and slivers of steel wool. Eyes and hands should also be protected when using mortar, because it contains hydrated lime which will cause burns. Poisonous, toxic, or inflammable materials should be securely stored. Lock up insecticides and

paint removers. Such potential hazards as oil-soaked rags should be burned immediately in an incinerator.

The first problem to study is structural decay. Structural decay is a complex phenomenon that is usually the result of several factors, but chief among these is moisture. Weather, the surrounding soil, possible substreams, atmospheric humidity, rising damp, or changes in the water table may all be factors. Human use or abuse over time may have taken their toll. Overloading of the building, mechanical vibration, excavations, and drains can also contribute to decay. Physical, chemical, and organic attack do their part as well.

The freeze-thaw cycle is the worst manifestation of physical attack. Moisture gets into foundations or walls, freezes, and continually dislodges pointing, stones, or bricks. The crystallization of soluble salts will cause similar destruction; they may be derived from the atmosphere, result from initial poor construction, bad earlier cleaning, or inadequate damp-proofing. Winter road and sidewalk salt is perhaps the worst present-day problem with which we are faced.

Major chemical attack, on the other hand, is most likely to occur in downtown urban areas where massive amounts of sulphur dioxide gases assault the actual make-up of stone and brick. Combined with rain and the moisture produced by the freeze-thaw cycle, this results in a constant and powerful barrage of sulphuric acid.

Weeds and ivy have a preference for growing in structural cracks. This organic attack dislodges pointing and allows moisture to get in.

From their conception, buildings begin to deteriorate. Moisture, the single most insidious and

The ruins of this nineteenth-century house still contain important details of period building practices.

destructive factor, can be divided into two categories, seepage and condensation. Seepage in this context is external moisture or water that has entered any portion of a building, although it is most common in the foundation area. Condensation results from the collision of hot and cold temperatures inside a structure. Dampness will occur due to either of these causes. An instant test for dampness is to tape a pocket mirror to the ceiling of the suspect room or basement. If it collects moisture, you have a dampness problem.

SEEPAGE: PROBLEMS AND REMEDIES

The foundation supports the rest of the structure, and it is as well to begin there with our remedial procedures. Water entering a building for any prolonged period of time will not only do surface damage, but in concert with other deteriorating agents or even by itself will also affect the structural integrity of the building. In the repair of structural defects, it is critical to repair the damage, rotted rafter ends for example, but it is even more important to find and remedy the cause of the problem. To prevent those rafter ends from rotting once more, repair the roof.

Broken eavestroughing, an often neglected and regular casualty of harsh northern climates, will eventually damage the foundation. Early homes frequently had cisterns in the basement to collect rainwater. Although these water supply systems have been for the most part abandoned, it is astonishing to still find them connected and overflowing in many basements. Wiser people did disconnect them, but this usually meant letting the pipes hang down the wall, continually soaking the wall, and

Clinging vines, although romantic and attractive, do cause deterioration.

seeping through the foundation into the cellar These same eavestroughs, even if in good condition, may fill up with branches, leaves, and other material. This causes water to back up resulting in roof penetration. Ice dams in winter are the worst example. As freezing and thawing cycles occur, ice builds up on the roof edge. When more melting snow runs down the roof, it hits this ice dam. The only course for water and ice is to back up under the shingles and come in through the roof.

Changes in landscape gradation over the life of the house will alter drainage patterns and can cause seepage problems. Whether in urban or rural situations, the chances are that your house is surrounded by one hundred years of rubble. This is one reason that early sketches, prints, or photographs of the building are so important, because you will be able to see just how the house was originally landscaped. Constant landscaping over the years, both in the city and the country, and sidewalk build-up in the city play an important part in changing the gradation of the land and its initial drainage patterns. Today, sidewalks are frequently above doorway entrances, allowing runoff to wash directly into them. In one particular example that comes to mind, a rural mill pond and its stream had been blocked by a new road that was constructed with inadequate drainage. It was no wonder that water flowed through the basement of the nearby one hundred and fifty-year-old house where none had been found before. The water was only taking the easiest path down the incline.

Changes in planting near the house will also contribute to alterations in drainage. Thirsty trees, for

*Movement in the outer walls, which
has been transferred to the main
beam, has resulted in the floor
joists coming loose from their pockets.*

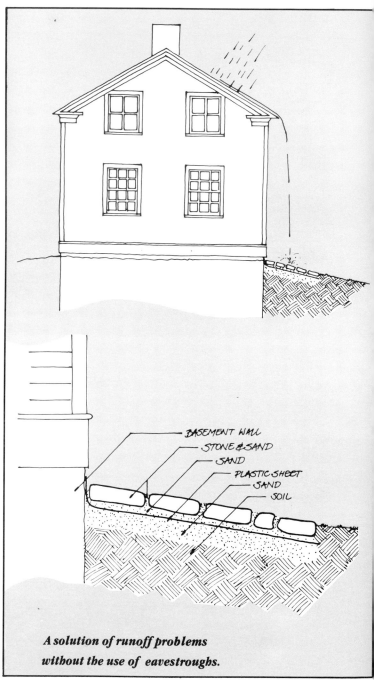

instance, sometimes dry out the soil, allowing settlement of a specific area. Again, water follows the path of least resistance.

Snow build-up and runoff are additional problems that may result in foundation-damaging seepage. The accumulation from snow clearance and roof build-up can lead to great piles of snow along the sides of the house. Come spring thaw, there is no adequate runoff. Subsequently, the basement fills up with water.

Moisture penetration is extremely commonplace in houses with rubble-stone foundations. Constant water contact leeches the lime out of the mortar, leaving only the sand. The foundation, in some cases, becomes basically a neatly stacked pile of stones with no real means of adhesion.

Past construction or remodeling will sometimes leave voids in the foundation. Areas where new

*A solution of runoff problems
without the use of eavestroughs.*

Heat cables on low-pitched roofs help prevent ice dams.

A new concrete foundation has been poured to replace the badly deteriorated original. The owner has kept some period detail by capping the new concrete with granite saved from the original foundation.

This basement entrance has suffered because of shoddy service installations and an inadequate attempt to close it up.

The sump pump is an efficient and cheap way to eliminate moisture in the basement.

pipes or wiring have been brought through an old wall are prime examples. A tradesman, in his haste to finish one job and get on to the next, may have failed to remortar or waterproof adequately around the opening he made. The results are obvious.

It is important to note that it is frequently impossible to stop the source of a water problem. Therefore, one must learn to reroute the moisture so as not to damage the structure. Immediate remedies include the repair of eavestroughs and gutters. Make sure that they drain away from the house. All areas where moisture can get in should be sealed. Where possible, grade away from the house. The archaeological importance of grading or the placement of vegetation as part of the period setting, however, may not make such changes feasible.

Due to economic and physical restraints, long-term stop-gap measures are commonly all that can be done to alleviate seepage problems in foundations, basements, or crawl spaces. A concrete slab in the basement or the installation of a sump pump may be the only answers.

Perhaps the most efficient method of moisture control in the period structure is the excavation and repair of the foundation. A rubble-stone foundation should then be pointed and parged. Once the foundation is tarred, weeping tiles should be placed around it, fill should be replaced and properly graded.

The basement of a period structure must often be enlarged to provide extra headroom or space for a new furnace. To do this without disturbing the original structure, one must either underpin or build a small concrete outcropping before pouring a concrete slab. When underpinning, care must be taken to excavate small areas at a time to prevent the origi-nal foundation from collapsing. Adequate moisture control procedures must be followed.

When dealing with any outside water problems, beware of inside treatments. There are no successful solutions, and you may end up causing more damage than you prevent.

CONDENSATION: PROBLEMS AND REMEDIES

Condensation is usually a more insidious problem than seepage, but it may be more easily solved. Inadequate ventilation, leaky plumbing, and improperly vented washers and dryers may all cause plaster to crumble, wallpaper to peel, and wood to rot. Solutions include plumbing repair, venting the basement, trimming vegetation around the house, and installing a dehumidifier or an electric fan to assist drying out the atmosphere.

Whenever you set about correcting either seepage or condensation, remember that the problem area will begin to dry out almost immediately. You are inviting insect infestation unless you coat all woodwork with a pentachlorophenol preservative.

FLOORS: HIGHS AND LOWS

The next area of noticeable defects in a house is usually the floors. Any bulges or bellies will be obvious to the eye or by checking paint drips and stains near baseboards. A surefire method of seeing how level your floors are is to place a marble in the center. If it doesn't get snagged on uneven floorboards, its path will indicate variations in height.

There are several reasons for crooked floors. Historically, undersized joists were sometimes used. Where a twelve-by-twelve beam enters a wall, it may

Although a large beam has been used, its effectiveness has been drastically reduced by the cutting of its ends for joints and wall intersections.

When removing walls or staircases, make sure that load bearing beams and joists are well supported.

When jacking unlevel floors, do it slowly, one or two turns per day, and stabilize rather than raise.

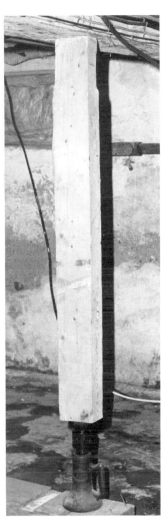

be cut down to a six-by-six. The beam is, in effect, doing the support work of a six-by-six. In combination with undersized joists, inadequate bridging frequently leads to excessive spring or complete failure of floor systems.

Beams (floor joists) may have deteriorated, causing floor defects. The ends may have rotted off where they have been set into masonry walls. Excessive condensation in the cellar or crawl space may give rise to wet rot, dry rot, or insect infestation. Any one of these situations, or a combination, may occur.

Human abuse over the years can also play a part in floor problems. Generations of plumbers, heating contractors, and electricians have cut through joists, putting the qualities of workmanship in their own trade ahead of the structural integrity of the whole house.

Jack posts that were installed early in the history of the house may have rotted at the base. In effect, they are not supporting the floor at all.

Once again it should be remembered that some of the reasons for buying an old house in the first place are the charms of its irregularities. Do you really want everything to be straight and true? Although the floors may not be entirely level, if you can find no deterioration in floor support systems,

any irregularities may merely be the ravages of old age. These may, in fact, be something to live with and enjoy rather than correct.

However, assuming that deterioration has occurred, all surrounding support systems must be examined and repaired. The problems that are causing the deterioration must be rectified, including those discussed in the previous section. Foundation walls may have to be repointed or proper drainage systems installed.

Where wooden posts have rotted out, new steel twist posts should be introduced. New post footings should be poured, the posts set into place, and *slowly*, over a period of weeks, the floor should be raised to as near its original level as possible. If this raising is done with haste, plaster will crack and

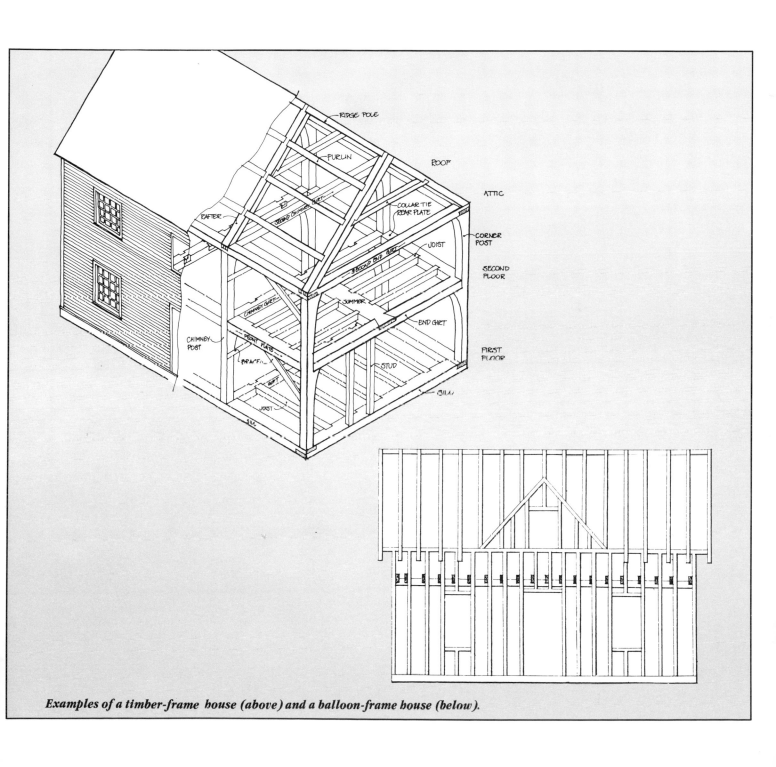

Labels on the timber-frame house (above):
RIDGE POLE
PURLIN
ROOF
ATTIC
COLLAR TIE
REAR PLATE
SECOND CHIMNEY GIRT
RAFTER
CORNER POST
JOIST
SECOND END GIRT
SECOND FLOOR
SUMMER
CHIMNEY GIRT
END GIRT
CHIMNEY POST
FRONT PLATE
BRACE
STUD
FIRST FLOOR
GIRT
SILL
JOIST
SILL

Examples of a timber-frame house (above) and a balloon-frame house (below).

Circular saw marks.   *Jack-plane marks.*   *Upright or pit saw marks.*

joinery areas (door frames, for example) will buckle and warp. It is often wise to add jack posts to beams where there is some doubt of their strength. These posts should not lift but merely help to distribute the load. Remember, though, that jack posts in the basement create obstacles in otherwise clear areas.

Where a beam has rotted off in a wall, it may be possible to shore it up with a jack post. If desirable, the rotten end can be cut off, and a new section spliced into it and set into the wall. Splicing new material into vandalized beams should also be done at this time. Rotten beam ends can also be stabilized *in situ* by the use of epoxies, although the specialized nature of this process and the cost are usually prohibitive for the private preservationist.

Undersized joists can be remedied by two methods. A new joist may be introduced to run at right angles to the existing joist; it is supported by jack posts and raised to the desired level. In balloon frame houses (see *Framing*, below), new bridgework can be added to the floor system.

FRAMING:
WHYS AND WHEREFORES

The use of wood in domestic architecture in North America can be traced back to the initial settlements of the Virginia and New England states. European timber-framing techniques were employed by these early builders, even to the point of using oak both in framing and cladding. Oak was commonly used in the Old Country, but it was extremely hard to work with the basic tools available to the settlers.

The frameworks of these timber buildings were frequently filled with brick (or noggin) infill. Over them was placed rough plank and narrow clapboard. This style of building carried right through the Atlantic seaboard into Canada. In Quebec, a similar method was called *colombage pierrotte*.

Around 1800, however, Henry Finkle, a member of the Canadian Corps of Engineers during the War of 1812, built a frame house using more easily worked native woods cut with whip and crosscut saws. This was the first such structure in the Kingston area and in the country.

In 1819, Andrew Bell, son of the important Canadian pioneer Reverend William Bell, wrote home to Scotland describing life in the new land. Among other things, he mentioned methods of clearing the land by means of oxen, the planting of native crops such as Indian corn, and the use of "a kind of bush called mouseweed, the back of which makes as good cordage as hemp."

The elder Bell divided one of his lots among four of his sons, and Andrew was soon busy planting his quarter with potatoes and Indian corn. He was not so busy, though, that he didn't have time to write of the houses in the new land:

The country houses are built of logs and covered with planks or bark of trees. The town houses are frames covered with planed boards, lapped over one another to send off the rain, and the roof is covered with pieces of wood about the size of slats. These are called shingles. Some houses are painted white, some yellow, some red. Provisions are cheap and wages high. . . . Tell my grandmother that we were never in better health, nor happier than we are now.[1]

By the end of the War of 1812, timber drives were a frequent occurrence on the Ottawa River, and as settlement grew, native woods were fully utilized using the new techniques employed by Henry Finkle.

A board and batten clad building. Ontario, mid-nineteenth century.

An example of carpenter ant deterioration.

Formal coursed ashlar facades were very prestigious, and wooden imitations such as this one attempted to capture some of their grandeur.

A mid-nineteenth-century wood
shingle clad house in Maine.

A wood shingle clad building in
Quebec, mid-nineteenth century.

A delightful clapboard house. New England, last quarter eighteenth century.

During this period, winters were spent cutting the primeval forest with felling axes and squaring the logs with broadaxes. In spring, the logs began their trip down the river. Alexander Caldwell, for example, started lumbering at age twelve. By age thirty-five, his family business was producing two to three hundred thousand board feet of lumber annually, as well as about thirty thousand squared logs. In 1842, John Gillies of Heron's Mills, Lanark County, Ontario, was selling pit-sawn lumber for six to eight dollars per thousand feet. The frame builder's history is closely tied to lumber production, and it can be divided into approximate dates when techniques changed:

1680-1840	Timber Framing
1800-1870	Braced Framing
1880-1930	Balloon Framing

Combinations or survivals of any one of these styles are still practised today.

It is important to note that the change from the colonist (handmade) structure, no matter what the technique, to machine-made components began between 1830 and 1850. The circular saw was introduced at that time giving rise to standardized lumber, and machine-made hardware and nails became readily available.

A frame building can be divided into three sections for the purposes of analysis and preservation: the framework, the sheathing or skin (nailed directly to the studs or quarters and rafters), and the cladding or siding. All lumber used for studding and sheathing was cut, and still is, in a plain-sawn method; all saw cuts are made in a single direction. Difficulties that may arise in a frame building often have to do with the fact that boards cut near the

*This 1860 house is clad in a later
(1920) tongue-and-groove siding.
Originally, clapboard probably
would have been used.*

outside of a log have a tendency to warp easily, because the cells on the outside of a tree contain more moisture than those on the inside.

Wood can be separated into two basic types, hardwood and softwood. Hardwood comes from broad leaf or deciduous trees, such as ash, oak, elm, walnut, or butternut. Evergreen or cone-bearing trees yield the softwoods: pine, fir, cedar, spruce, and redwood.

Framework techniques have already been listed, and sheathing methods require little explanation. The cladding or siding, on the other hand, was applied in a variety of styles that require some definition. Clapboard refers to planks nailed horizontally, one overlapping the other. Bevel siding is similar, but the profiles differ somewhat. Board and batten cladding is made up of vertical planks, butt-joined, with the batten nailed over the joint. Tongue-and-groove siding is matched; there is no overlap. Slate and wood shingle cladding appeared in the latter part of the 1600s, after the arrival of clapboard.

When approaching a timber structure as a preservationist, a thorough and full survey must be carried out. The method is the same as when looking for moisture problems. Symptoms and signs must be carefully searched out and recognized for what they are. Trace defects and causes from the symptoms.

Every timber that is buried in a wall must be carefully examined (beam ends, floor joists, bond timbers). Do not trust apparently hard outer faces; probe and test for moisture content that would favor decay and insect attack.

Check timber lintels that are showing, as well as places where they might be hidden in masonry. Lintels can become deformed, causing local cracks to open in the adjacent structure. Cracks may admit water and then decay might commence in the lintel.

Look carefully at the backs of door linings and the backs of sash window frames. Rot and insect attack can occur in such hidden favorable environments.

Hunt for areas that could be affected by water entering through cracks in external walls.

Examine all timbers near the ground; they can be attacked by rising damp. Also, test all timbers in contact with the ground: ground plates or sills, door sills, floor joists, and column bases.

Check all wood which may be affected by leaks in the roof. Watch for water stains and traces of mould on the inside of the roof.

Look at all the places where water might sit on ledges or in cracks. Horizontal surfaces and horizontal checks and splits in exposed timbers should all be suspect.

Test any places where softwood may have been used. These include lath, battens, floor, and roof boarding. Many voracious insects specialize in attacking sapwood.

Probe all joints, crevices, and rough timber surfaces; beetles will lay their eggs there.

Potential trouble spots occur in exposed timbers which can suffer from abrasion: door sills, doors, frames, corner posts—any locations where there might be a lot of pedestrian or vehicle traffic.

All fixed furniture that may be in contact with damp floors or walls must be examined, including lined cupboards and paneling. Special care must be taken to survey this type of woodwork in basements.

Look for signs of unventilated spaces beneath wooden floors at ground level. Blocked vents and earth piled against external walls to or above ground floor level can cause problems.

A rubble-stone house in the style of Quebec's French Regime. It could have been built any time between 1670 and 1770.

Check infill panels in half-timber structures and horizontal log fill between uprights. Infill panels may crack away from the main structure because of differential expansion and other movement. Such cracks will admit water.

Insect infestation is a common problem in the early house. Remedial procedures, when structural damage has not occurred, can be carried out by the judicious use of readily available but extremely poisonous chemicals. Chlordane and pentachlorophenol will effectively eliminate most common insect problems. Vehicles, such as methyl hydrate or varsol, may be used with these chemicals, either for injection into the infected area or application with an ordinary paintbrush. If you are repairing woodwork with new lumber, make sure it is pretreated.

Be wary of open joints in timber structures, but *do not wedge them up or fill them with inelastic materials*. Changes in humidity may cause them to close again, and serious damage may occur if the wood is prevented from attaining its original dimensions. Joints may be strained, mortise and tenon joints smashed, and pegs and pins may snap unless proper care is exercised. Use elastic gap sealants for temporary repairs, but remember they do not last forever. If rubber, plastic, or other forms of gap sealants have been used in the past, check their performance. They may have failed, and water may again be entering the structure.

Watch for metals in contact with hardwoods like oak. Tannic acid attacks lead and will perforate lead flashing or roof sheathing. Iron and steel can corrode in these circumstances.

THE STRUCTURE   91

Defects can occur where the roof is penetrated by some architectural feature. Look for water stains anywhere near roofing, rainwater pipes and gutters, flashing, copings, parapets, chimneys, and dormers.

Carefully examine junctions between different structures: house and summer kitchen, house and porch, original building, and later additions. Different foundations may lead to differential movement and the development of cracks that overstress structural timbers or admit water.

Check timbers or woodwork that may be exposed to high temperatures, such as next to heating units or electric light bulbs.

The house you are preserving may not have a timber frame, with all the cracks and joints that implies, it may be stone, brick, or even solid log. It is safe to assume, however, that wood will have been used to a large extent. The enemies are moisture, rot, and insects. When surveying wooden components, be suspicious of everything. Water damage will occur where it is hardest to find, and insects will burrow to the most unlikely and unreachable places. It will do little good to restore the interior of a house when the superstructure has been undermined.

MASONRY: STONE AND BRICK

The evolution of the masonry structure in North America came about more as a result of the availability of craftsmen and raw materials than as a quest to follow particular fashions. Stone and brick buildings are highly prized by the preservationists of today for their age, style, and appearance, but they require particular kinds of attention to insure that they will remain sound.

The powder magazine at Port Royal in Annapolis, Nova Scotia, dates from about 1708 and is reputed to be one of the earliest stone structures in Canada.[2] The somewhat later river settlements of Quebec and eastern Ontario are dominated by such structures. In fact, the use of stone in houses was more widespread than brick. Diverse ethnic groups, ranging from the Dutch of the Hudson Valley, through the Swiss Mennonites of Lancaster County, Pennsylvania, to the Germans in Delaware, employed various forms of rubble-stone construction. Some of these forms seem to have been used by more than one group. There is considerable similarity between the Germanic cottage (*Kuche-Stuberammer*) and the basic French-Canadian house described in Jean Palardy's *The Furniture of French Canada*.[3]

Scottish masons were present during the initial settlement of Perth, Ontario, as recorded by Robert Gourlay in July of 1817: "William Spalding, a mason, from Dundee Parish, Forfar County, Scotland. Wife and 1 child left at home. Has erected a house 26 x 19 feet."[4] It has been said[5] that it was in Scotland, not in England, that the Classical Revival had its largest success and longest life. Perhaps this explains in part the glowing legacy left by Scottish masons in the new land.

Early documents relating to stone buildings in New Jersey refer to the fact that the walls were claybound using chopped straw. Later, in both stone and brick construction, a soft mortar made from a mixture of lime and sand was used. Limestone (calcium carbonate) was burnt and quick-lime remained. Mussel, oyster, and clam shells also contain lime and were frequently used with quick-lime to make mortar.

The burning of limestone was practised by Samuel Strickland in Ontario around 1840. He calculated that he would need nearly one hundred bushels of lime to plaster his walls and build his chimneys, so an immense pile of the largest logs available was constructed.

The timber from half an acre was needed to build the heap, on top of which a log framework was built to hold the limestone. Twenty cartloads of stone were then drawn to the log-heap and placed within the frame after being broken into small pieces with a sledge hammer. The fire was then lit, and the pile burned during the night; but the intense heat of the coals prevented the lime being removed until a week had passed. It was then collected and covered, but it was impossible to eliminate entirely small pieces of unburnt stone, which detracted from the value of the lime as plaster.[6]

Most stone houses that we are familiar with today fall into the following categories: *uncoursed rubble-stone*, common field-stone, sometimes roughly dressed; *coursed rubble-stone*, same as the uncoursed type but constructed in a more uniform manner; *ashlar*, so called when the outside facing stone is cut, not roughly dressed; *coursed ashlar*, uniform stonework, almost like large brickwork; and *broken ashlar*, a type having no continuous horizontal joints as in coursed ashlar.

When approaching the stone house, the preservationist should be aware that it may suffer from the problems already discussed in this chapter, but because of its make-up it is perhaps more susceptible to certain aspects of these problems. Both settlement and inadequate drainage may damage the structural integrity of the building. Human abuse to the stone or joints, such as stucco, moved openings, or poor repointing can require extensive repair.

Repointing is probably the single most important job that will have to be done. It becomes necessary for a number of reasons, including worn-out original pointing, loose stones, moisture traps, and interior drafts. To point a rubble-stone house, all the joints must be cut back at least one-half inch. New mortar of the same composition, color, and texture must be used. Remember that mortar was lime-based and quite soft when the house was built, because it allowed the stone to move without breaking. For the most part, the traditional mix was four parts lime to twelve parts sand. Today, a good durable mix to use is three parts mason's lime and one part white medusa to twelve parts sand. This formula provides all the necessary features: it has good working qualities, is stiff but malleable, reasonable

A beehive brick kiln. Hamilton, Ontario, 1914.

An early Tyndall stone quarry. East Selkirk, Manitoba, circa 1890.

UNCOURSED RUBBLE WORK

COURSED RUBBLE

BROKEN ASHLAR

COURSED ASHLAR

RANDOM COURSED

Stone types and building styles.

in cost, readily available, and has the same physical qualities (texture and color) as the original. Mortar should never be stronger than the adjoining stones; *never use straight Portland cement*, it is too hard for most stone structures. As a final note on mixing mortars, the sand that is used must be clean, dry, and fine.

Mortar joints decay because the original mortar (or an early replacement) was too strong, because of poor pointing techniques, or due to natural weathering. These problems will probably result in moisture penetration, frost action, the growth of vegetation, or a combination of the three.

Pointing should be done all at once with a minimum crew of three people: one to mix, one to carry, and one to point. For example, chip out a complete wall and then point it. Patch pointing is unsatisfactory, because it tends to weather at a

different rate than the rest of the wall. Rake out the joints, then clean and wash down the area. Point with the mortar described above. The job should be commenced early in the day and halted in the early afternoon. By that time the mortar will have stiffened but not adhered to the stone, and the tooling or rubbing down of the joints can take place. It is imperative that any sand used in the pointing process be obtained from the same pit in order to keep the color consistent. It may be possible to determine where the original sand was quarried; if so, try to obtain sand from that location.

One cannot become a stonemason capable of building an entire wall by reading a book. However, the nature of rubble-stone construction lends itself to minor structural repairs by the novice mason. The rubble-stone wall is, in fact, made up of two walls, an inner and an outer, with the middle space

or cavity filled with rip-rap and mortar. Occasionally, the cavity is left empty, and sometimes, as in the walls of Quebec City, it is filled with earth. Headers or bondstones may stretch from side to side, although in the Rideau Corridor they do not appear commonly, a peculiar phenomenon that arose because the Scottish masons of the area, renowned for their skill and expertise, did not find them necessary.

Before beginning work, make sure that the foundation is adequate. The footings of most stone houses of the 1800s were merely pads six inches to a foot wider than the foundation on which they sat. If there is a support problem, you must rebuild in stone or pour concrete footings.

Arrange stones on both sides of the wall to be built or repaired. Remember that large stones are hard to pick up; put them on the bottom layers. Of course, you may not be able to do this because of the size of the stones used in surrounding or adjoining walls.

When repairing a wall, strike a line between a point on the existing wall and points you are to repair. Having done that, lay down a bed of soft mortar approximately six inches back from the line. When the stone is placed on the mortar, it will spread the mortar close to the line and space will be left for pointing to be done later.

Lay up your first course (this is what a row of stones is called) on one side of the wall, then proceed in the same manner on the other side. Fill up the cavity between with mortar and rubble-stone. Start on course two using the same procedures but make sure these new stones fall over the cracks of course one and so on. Always "eyeball" the wall you are working on from the sides, front and, if possible,

The mason is pointing a rubble-stone wall. He applies a stiff mortar to a raked joint, and after letting it set, rubs the joints flush with a clean, dry burlap sack.

View of a rubble-stone wall from above, showing the interior wall (right), exterior wall (left) and the rubble-filled cavity (center).

from the top as well. The irregularity of rubble-stone makes illusion very possible. Without constant checking you are liable to build outward, inward, or in a wavy pattern. Try to make sure that your face stones have a somewhat rectangular quality, and never build more than two courses on one side at a time.

Although the use of brick in domestic architecture was less widespread than stone, it has been recorded[7] that skilled brickmakers from Holland had established kilns in New Amsterdam as early as 1628 and were manufacturing bricks in several shapes and colors. In the initial settlement group at Jamestown in 1607, bricklayers were listed among the tradesmen.[8] Little remains of Jamestown today, but the skill of these early bricklayers is still visible in the early capital buildings in Williamsburg. Other examples of a high degree of craftsmanship in brick construction are to be found in Maryland and the Hudson Valley.

While common in North America from an early date, the first brick house in Ontario is probably the Bergers' House in Belleville, erected in 1794. Brick was commonly used in the Niagara area from the turn of the nineteenth century, and the counties of York, Durham and Ontario list brick buildings in the local architectural inventories of 1845.

It is often difficult to determine where the actual bricks originated, but in one particular case the facts are clear. Also in 1845, a farmhouse was built in Scugog Township, near present-day Port Perry, Ontario. The land surrounding Old Reach, as it was called, is a rich clay-loam, and the Scottish masons employed in constructing the building obtained their materials from a pit dug behind the house. No doubt, a temporary kiln was built on the site.[9]

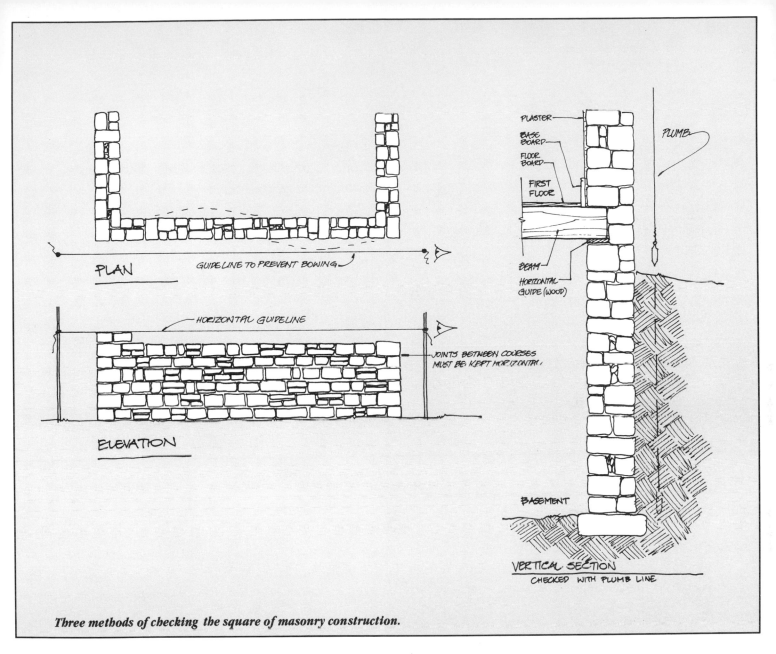

PLAN

GUIDE LINE TO PREVENT BOWING

HORIZONTAL GUIDELINE

JOINTS BETWEEN COURSES MUST BE KEPT HORIZONTAL

ELEVATION

PLASTER

BASE BOARD

FLOOR BOARD

FIRST FLOOR

BEAM

HORIZONTAL GUIDE (WOOD)

PLUMB

BASEMENT

VERTICAL SECTION

CHECKED WITH PLUMB LINE

Three methods of checking the square of masonry construction.

Despite the fact that nine bricklayers are mentioned in the 1857 census of Cobourg, Ontario, brick construction in this area had only just come into its own by this date. In fact, brick manufacturing remained somewhat primitive (hand-done) until the mid-nineteenth century. The benefits to the brick-manufacturing industry rendered by the Industrial Revolution are perhaps best portrayed by an investigation of the _Don Valley Pressed Brick Works Catalogue_ of 1894 which contains a large array of ready-made goods.

The preservationist who is approaching a brick building is in much the same situation as one owning a stone house. Again, repointing is the single most important job to be done and similar procedures should be followed using the same durable

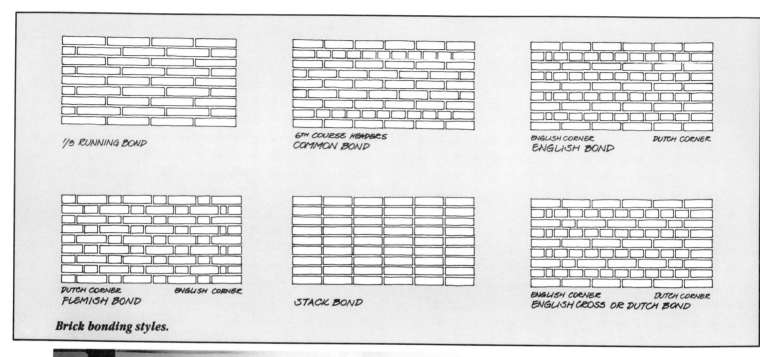

1/3 RUNNING BOND

6TH COURSE HEADERS
COMMON BOND

ENGLISH CORNER   DUTCH CORNER
ENGLISH BOND

DUTCH CORNER   ENGLISH CORNER
FLEMISH BOND

STACK BOND

ENGLISH CORNER   DUTCH CORNER
ENGLISH CROSS OR DUTCH BOND

Brick bonding styles.

This Loyalist house in the Rideau corridor (second quarter nineteenth century) is built of locally manufactured brick and tooled stone. The masons who built it were probably employed by Colonel By in the construction of the Rideau Canal during the 1820s.

Two treatments of urban Victorian housing; the one on the right has been cleaned, the one on the left has been repainted. The painted house, although not as aesthetically appealing, will probably be in better condition in twenty years.

The Flemish bond style of brickwork used in the construction of this mid-nineteenth-century farmhouse follows the Dutch tradition started two hundred years earlier.

Efflorescence often appears after chemical cleaning. It will disappear within six months to a year with natural weathering. Moisture on sidewalks and walls will carry winter salt up into masonry materials and also cause efflorescence.

An example of brick spalling due to condensation and the freeze-thaw cycle.

Brick deterioration caused by inadequate gutter maintenance. Notice the tooled quoins.

but elastic mortar formula. Any structural defects should be corrected first.

It is important that new mortar match the color and texture of the existing material, and this may be achieved by the sand used and possibly by adding old lumps of lime to the mix. Falling mortar, loose bricks, and damp walls are the tell-tale signs that repointing is necessary.

Joints should be cut back to a minimum of one inch. Extreme care is needed not to damage the edges of the bricks, and the joints should be carefully raked by hand. Large voids should be filled in first; several thin layers are better than a single thick one. Lay the mortar in the joint, brush the excess from the bricks (a stiff bristle brush is good for this), and wait until firm but not hard to do your tooling. Efflorescence will disappear with natural weathering.

As in stone repointing, always work in moderate temperatures, with a minimum crew of three, when there is no danger of frost. Hot sun will cause the mortar to dry too quickly, and rain will result in staining from the lime. Never use antifreezes in the pointing mixture.

The procedures used in cleaning both stone and brick are basically the same. The five common methods are: washing, abrasive blasting, wet blasting, mechanical cleaning, and chemical cleaning. Each one has distinct advantages and disadvantages.

Washing involves the use of water sprayed under low pressure in conjunction with bristle brushes. This method is cheap, quiet, and results in relatively little debris around the site. The disadvantages are that only surface dirt is removed and there is the possibility of moisture damage if the pointing is in poor condition.

Cleaning brick using sulphuric acid and washing with water under high pressure.

Loss of detail due to sandblasting.

Dry sandblasting on a rubble-stone house.

Loss of detail due to sandblasting.

Abrasive blasting or sandblasting is done with compressed air and grit. There is no moisture penetration problem here; it is fast and effective in removing stubborn discoloration and paints. The risks involved include the danger of damage to stone surfaces (original tool marks or relief from detailed stone) and the destruction of the outer skin of brick. The process is both dirty and noisy; in downtown areas permits are required and adequate insurance is needed.

Wet blasting is fundamentally the same as the abrasive kind, except that water is added to the equation. This is less abrasive than dry blasting, no dust is created, but the runoff will make quite a mess at the bottom of the wall. Depending on the condition of the pointing, moisture penetration can occur.

Grinding tools and brushes are used in mechanical cleaning. This is a dry process, so no water problems will arise. It is costly and time-consuming, however, and one runs the risk of losing details from the surfaces cleaned.

Chemical cleaning is done with a combination of water and acid which is brushed on and washed off. This process will remove substances that no other method will. It is relatively fast and not cost-prohibitive. The use of acids requires that care be exercised for the safety of the workers. Unless a complete chemical analysis of the building is made, there is a possibility of long-term deterioration in either stone or brick. (If the house is painted, what kind is it? What type of mortar is used?) Chemical cleaning must be professionally done. There is considerable danger of damage to vegetation from runoff. Overspray will affect paint on cornices, stone window details, and so on.

Most preservationists would like to remove weather stains and paint from these surfaces, but careful consideration is needed before choosing a cleaning method. Even if you decide to do the work yourself, it would be worthwhile to consult someone knowledgeable in the field. An expert must be called in when dealing with special problems like graffiti, oil stains, and metal stains.

LOG BUILDINGS

The folk legends of North America are replete with stories of life in the little log cabin, and the new-found interest in these simple structures will no doubt raise their stature in the history of North American architecture. Academically speaking, the log house or log cabin was bypassed, because it was always thought to be merely temporary shelter until something more substantial was erected. Common in Scandinavia from the eleventh century, Swedes and Finns are thought to be the originators of log construction on this continent. Scandinavian settlers on Delaware Bay in 1638 erected weatherproof homes using squared logs caulked with moss, straw, and mud. Log homes were also built by Germanic groups in eighteenth-century Pennsylvania, and their proximity to other ethnic groups led to a profusion of log buildings throughout North America. Germanic settlers were the source for log-building techniques among both English-speaking settlers and the military who built both garrisons and blockhouses in this manner.

The log cabin, a crude temporary shelter, gave way to the more complex log house, a structure which in some cases followed the rudimentary "Frontier Georgian" style of the times. By 1800, the log house was common throughout North America. It provided a cheap, efficient, easily built home. By the 1920s, though, log houses were no longer being constructed, because of the lack of logs with sufficient dimensions, and more accurately because they were too unsophisticated for a nation weaned on, "How do you keep them down on the farm after they've seen Paree?"

Nevertheless, log houses possess a special charm and rustic appeal that have caused their resurgence in recent years. Due to the fact that it was often the first or perhaps the second structure to be erected on a farm, with newer buildings located nearby, as often as not log houses must be moved to an alternate site. Whether the log house is to be worked on *in situ* or moved, the basic problem-solving approach discussed in this section remains the same.

Moving a log house presents special difficulties in which the record-keeping abilities of the preservationist will be taxed to the utmost. Nowhere is the accuracy of the recording process more important than in this situation. Although the log house is a very basic form of jigsaw puzzle, the pieces are not as clearly marked as might be thought at first and they cannot be interchanged. A drawing must be made of each wall, indicating the number of logs (usually eleven in a one-and-a-half storey building). Each wall must be photographed, and then each log in that wall must be tagged with folding, waterproof metal tags. (Can lids can be used.) These tags are coded for each wall and the code transferred to the drawing of that wall. Overall measurements need to be taken, including the roof pitch and the positions of windows, doors, etc.

If the interior is to be restored with relative accuracy, all of its components must be numbered,

tagged, and the results transferred to a floor plan. It cannot be stressed enough how important this stage is both for the interior and the exterior. Two days spent on extra tagging at one end of the job will save two weeks of laborious sorting at the other.

In the disassembly process, try to follow the building of the house backwards. Begin with mouldings, door frames, doors, stair-rails, and windows. Move on to partitions and cabinets, then begin on the roof. The floors and staircase are next, and finally the actual logs should be removed.

The floors, staircase, and logs are most efficiently dealt with when the machinery you are using is on the site. A boom truck is probably the best choice for cost and expediency.

The top logs will be pinned through to the first two or three courses with hardwood pins or metal dowels. Have the boom truck lift the log slightly, so these can be pried out with crowbars. Often, time will have swelled wooden pins, and they must be cut with a chainsaw. Working systematically around the house, the boom truck should place the long logs on the truck bed, leaving the shorter ones on the ground for easy loading later. Easy access to all four walls at ground level is necessary at this time. Remember that although the boom truck is on an hourly rate and minutes will seem to take the form of dollar signs, care is essential, and the operator's sensitivity will save you time and material during the reassembly process.

The illustrations used here of the reassembly process will give a clear idea of how it is done. A footing and foundation has already been prepared in this example, an eighteen-inch wide concrete pad with a twelve-inch concrete block wall set on top of it. Bedrock is only twenty inches below ground level; if it were deeper, a wider pad would be used.

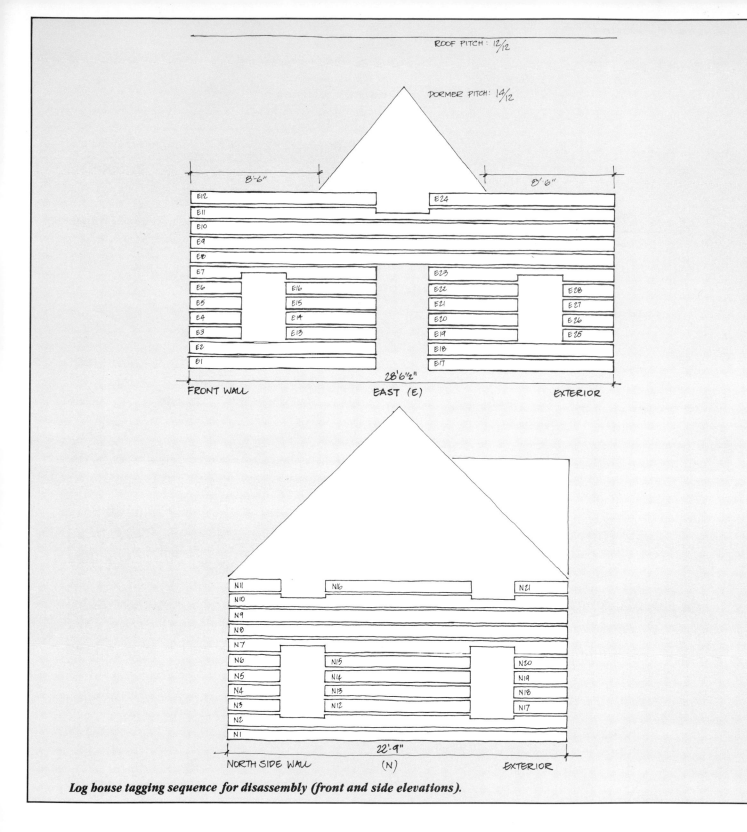

Log house tagging sequence for disassembly (front and side elevations).

This log house is standing on its original site. It was built about 1915 in Lanark County, Ontario.

Before any work begins, metal tags are attached to each individual log. Walls are lettered north, south, east and west, then each log is numbered in each wall. For example, the south wall logs would be s1, s2, and so on.

Accurate measuring is also necessary. Be sure to take overall measurements as well as those between openings.

Careful disassembly is important to prevent breakage and costly replacements.

Original windows can often be
used in the restoration.

A sensitive boom truck operator
will be able to lift the logs out of
position carefully.

Footings should already be poured
at the new location.

Unloading at the new site should
be done as carefully as possible.

The logs should be unloaded and stacked wall by wall.

Checking the metal tags at the new site.

Base logs are put in position on the new foundation.

Follow your numbering system in reassembly. Note the strapping of logs between windows.

The roof is assembled as it originally was.

Plywood sheathing and asphalt shingles are contemporary, cost-efficient compromises for twentieth-century living.

In the traditional manner, wood chinking is inserted between the logs.

*Chinking mortar is applied and
tooled on a slight angle to allow
rain runoff.*

This is also why a crawl space is being used, rather than a basement. The truck is unloaded in a systematic way, the reverse of loading procedures. Windows have already been taken to a shop for repair and reglazing. The components are stacked in order of precedence for the reassembly process. Wet rot has occurred in two of the base logs, and two new logs are cut to their dimensions (recorded on your wall plan) and placed. Dovetails are cut on location to get a perfectly accurate profile.

Once the initial sorting has been accomplished, the boom truck can return to place the logs in their original positions. Dovetails keep the long logs on a horizontal profile, while dovetail and saddle is used on short logs. Two-by-fours strap short fill-logs (those between doors and windows) to prevent them toppling over during reassembly. It is impera-

tive that the outside dimensions be continually checked; any discrepancy between the bottom long logs and the top long logs will prevent the top ones from fitting. Until the top logs are pinned, and in fact even until the roof and floor have been rebuilt, the entire structure will seem very wobbly and unsound.

Rafters for the roof and joists for the floor can now be put into position. In this case, new two-by-eight rafters are added to accommodate insulation and six-by-six floor beams for greater structural support. While these procedures are taking place, stage one of rechinking can commence. The photographs illustrate the traditional method. Split cedar rails are nailed between the logs in such a way as to allow the chinking to be applied over them on a slight angle to allow water runoff. The chinking is the same mortar mix described earlier in this chapter under stone and brick repointing.

When the major structural components are in place, including the floors and the roof, and the danger of major vibration is over, the second and final stage of chinking can begin. Traditionally, the mortar was frequently applied with a cedar shingle, used something like a paddle, and then it was smoothed. Log houses often move, so it is important to use a flexible mortar, otherwise a yearly maintenance problem may occur. One log house I know of was chinked five years ago using the flexible, durable mortar described in this chapter and has yet to need any repairs.

Whether the house you are dealing with is frame, stone, brick, or log, and whether you are repairing defects, preventing new ones, cleaning it, or moving it, remember that it existed for a long time before

The finished house on its new site.

you became involved. You are attempting to do two things: provide an enjoyable, adequate living space and preserve a structure that is worth preserving. Neither of these things will be assisted by haste. Take sufficient time to consider consequences and alternatives; your ancestors worked quickly but with great care, so should you. Presumably, you will be living for many tomorrows with what you have done today, and future generations will thank you for your care.

CHAPTER SIX

The Exterior

WHEN DEALING WITH THE EXTERIOR of a period house, one might dwell on these words of wisdom by an anonymous Chinese poet:

The facade of a building does not belong to only those who own it but all who behold it.

The restoration or rehabilitation of the exterior affects how the building will sit in its landscape and how it is viewed by passersby. As such, the themes created in it and its condition are an extremely significant part of the integrity of the entire structure.

Perhaps the most interesting part of an exterior wall is its fenestration, the distribution and arrangement of windows, doors, and ornamental trim. In many cases, it is these things that provide style to the building and the themes that are followed through in the interior. In a front elevation view, it is important to remember that the roof comprises approximately one-third of what the viewer sees. Flat roofs are an obvious exception, but since this element is ordinarily so prominent, it becomes almost as significant as fenestration in restoration or rehabilitation. Porches or verandahs were frequently added later in the history of a house. Because they were built with less attention to longevity than other parts, more thorough but less immediate attention may be necessary than with other exterior elements.

Preserving the exterior is an exercise which uses all the procedures that have been discussed thus far. Care must be taken to make repairs and changes that do not intrude on the building's original thematic integrity, while attention must be paid to eliminating current problems and preventing new ones that may be created by the special demands of modern technologies.

WINDOWS

The window in America was initially merely a hole in the wall with usually a shutter or some form of drape over it. I have heard two attractive definitions of the word: wind-door, an appropriate enough term, and wind-eye, a term perhaps more suited to vision or light in the interior of the house. In North America, oiled paper was used for the first window-panes. A particular kind of paper was ordered from England, and upon arrival in the colonies it was treated with linseed oil or animal grease to give it a somewhat transparent quality. These were called paper lights. It can be assumed that these panes were a most welcome relief from the almost black interiors that the early settlers knew.

Glass was a luxury in Europe throughout the 1600s, but its introduction to the new land came at an early stage. In 1608, settlers in Jamestown listed eight Polish and Dutch glass-makers who tried but failed in the making of glass.[1] By the mid-1600s some colonial timber-frame dwellings had casement windows in which small lozenge-shaped or rectangular pieces of glass, called quarries, were leaded together by means of cames. These cames would later become what we call munton bars in a double-hung window, although leaded quarries largely disappeared during the Revolutionary War when the metal was used to make musket shot.

During the 1600s, most glass still came from Europe. It was heavy in shipping, but it packed well, and good tariff rates made it a desirable import. This early glass was called Crown glass. It was blown by the glassmaker using a hollow tube. The bubble of glass at the end of the iron would have its end cut off, and the iron would be spun, centrifugal force creating a flat glass disc four or five feet in

A dilapidated twelve-over-eight sash window shows many of the problems that occur in period sashes. The glazing points are actually small, hand-forged nails.

This Nova Scotian house illustrates the importance of style, form, and texture when restoring or considering changes.

This is a good example of a new window unit in the same style as the original (circa 1835).

Old window units can be rebuilt, saving money and retaining important period details.

A new unit designed to fit a Victorian opening.

A Georgian-style window with elegant tracery, 1770-1780.

diameter. Small panes would be cut from this disc, and the center section, where the pontil iron was attached to the disc, would have a raised portion appropriately named the bull's-eye.

By 1700 hot glass was being blown into an elongated tube. Both ends were cut off, and the cylinder was reheated, slit from end to end and rolled out to form one large pane of glass. It was sometimes full of streaks, a little less brilliant than earlier types, but the process was standardized throughout North America. The dimensions of this glass governed the proportions of windows and transoms.

In 1825, Nathaniel Mallory set up practice on a site that is now known as Mallorytown, Ontario. From that date until 1840 his glassworks was employed in the manufacture of glassware for home utensils and construction. The Mallorytown glassworks and similar operations in Ontario and New Brunswick were only poor cousins to the early industries in Quebec. From 1845 to the epoch of the Victorian era, Quebec's glassworks dominated the production of residential and commercial building glass. As we consider an "antique" to be something one hundred years old or older, it is safe to assume that most glass found in the period home in eastern Canada came from Lower Canada.

By 1883, the Pittsburgh Glass Company had succeeded in producing plate glass in a profitable manner. It was at this time that leaded art glass (or stained glass as it is sometimes called) came into vogue.

Two distinct elements of deterioration to windows can occur: vandalism and moisture. In vandalism the obvious becomes fact. Just as the weather vane on the barn provides a tempting target for would-be marksmen, so an abandoned house and all those nice panes of glass become prey to rock throwers bent on improving their accuracy. Not only is the glass destroyed, but often finely profiled muntons are broken, requiring major surgery to the entire sash rather than the replacement of one or two panes. The vandalism of neglect is also rampant in the abandoned house. Vegetation has been allowed to grow up and beat against the sash. The constant battering of loose shutters may have broken lights or the sash. Years of slipshod patchwork or repairs and paint accumulation retard the preservationist in his resurrection of the window.

Moisture is an equally insidious enemy. Rain beating on a nine-over-nine window lends a sense of melancholy to the day, and its presence also has a sad effect on the improperly maintained window unit. Moisture around joints where there is insufficient caulking, as in glass-munton joints, or where glue has failed, as in frame construction, are perfect havens for wet rot to begin. The most prevalent area for this to occur is in the sill. Water penetration in the joints surrounding the actual window unit are also subject to this kind of attack. This is especially common in stone buildings where the stone-wood joint caulking has failed due to differential movement and temperature changes.

Dry rot is also a possibility. The space between a latched shutter and the box mechanism of the sash assembly is frequently susceptible to this form of deterioration.

Windows constitute a large portion of the house's appearance and absorb a large amount of capital for repair or replacement, so it is advisable to thoroughly examine the units during the initial inspection of the structure. Do the windows belong to the period, or are they later replacements? What type of

glazing has been used? What is the availability of replacement glass? How many lights are broken? Can the sashes be repaired, partially repaired, or do you require entirely new units? Do they fit? Often one may see a great pile of storm windows stacked in the basement, only to find on acquiring the property that the previous owner went to auctions and bought storm windows for reasons known only to him.

Although specific window deterioration may be due to moisture and vandalism, interrelated structural problems such as sagging and settlement will have a large effect on the window's operation. It commonly happens that a window in a sagging wall is removed for restoration. Before its removal, the window might have worked perfectly and needed only minor repairs. When the sash is replaced, all

newly glued and shipshape, it will neither fit the irregular opening nor function properly.

Obviously, windows are of paramount importance not only to prevent further deterioration in the rest of the structure, but also to enhance the overall appearance of the building. It is important from the outset to deal with windows in your flow chart and budget plan. The average replacement cost of a six-over-six window unit with storm and screen is two hundred and fifty dollars. On this premise, a one-and-a-half storey house requiring replacement of its twelve units would require an outlay of three thousand dollars.

Total replacement is a drastic measure that must be carefully weighed. Fortunately, it is often possible to repair window units so that they will function well and exclude the elements. To preserve the

build-up, it may be advisable to strip the sash completely. A sash in relatively good condition should be sanded, reglazed where necessary, reputtied, and repainted. However, when the entire unit has been stripped, first treat the raw wood with pentachlorophenol, then replace the glass, add new glazier's points, and reputty. It is important when reputtying to strike clean, precise angles. A simple procedure list to follow is: remove putty and points, replace glass, add points, reputty and repaint.

Paint used on windows should lap the glass and be trimmed back to give a weatherproof seal. When cutting new glass for an opening, always cut one-eighth of an inch smaller than the opening. If old glass is being used, allow for fifty per cent breakage in the cutting process – if you need one pane, get two.

The old lead putty will frequently adhere to old glass taken out of original frames. Domestic oven cleaner applied and left standing for a time in conjunction with scraping and washing will assist the cleaning process. A heat gun will also remove old putty, but more breakage will occur.

Dirt from years of neglect may have become ingrained in the glass. A combination of zero-zero-zero steel wool, straight ammonia, and a fair amount of rubbing should remove this grime. After the initial cleaning, rinse with plain water, then dry and polish with newspaper.

Like it or not, a new window unit is frequently the only solution to the problem. Whether it follows the design and construction of the original or whether it is made in sympathy with the rest, its installation can be quite simple. First, remove the existing window and surrounding frame, leaving the rough win-

frame, first clean and scrape loose paint, gluing or renailing where necessary, and then caulk the joints between the unit and the framework or cladding of the building. Make sure that the sill has a downward pitch with a drip to allow water runoff. If the sill is heavily weathered, sand and fill cracks with an epoxy or linseed oil/putty combination. Apply a preservative, such as pentachlorophenol, to raw wood to prevent insect attack. When painting, use two primer coats and one or two finish coats. Before painting, make sure that the underneath and sides of the sill have been well caulked.

Sash repair is a somewhat more complicated procedure. Remove the sash from the window opening, which should then be covered with plastic. Cleaning and scraping should eliminate loose paint, but if moulding details are completely lost due to paint

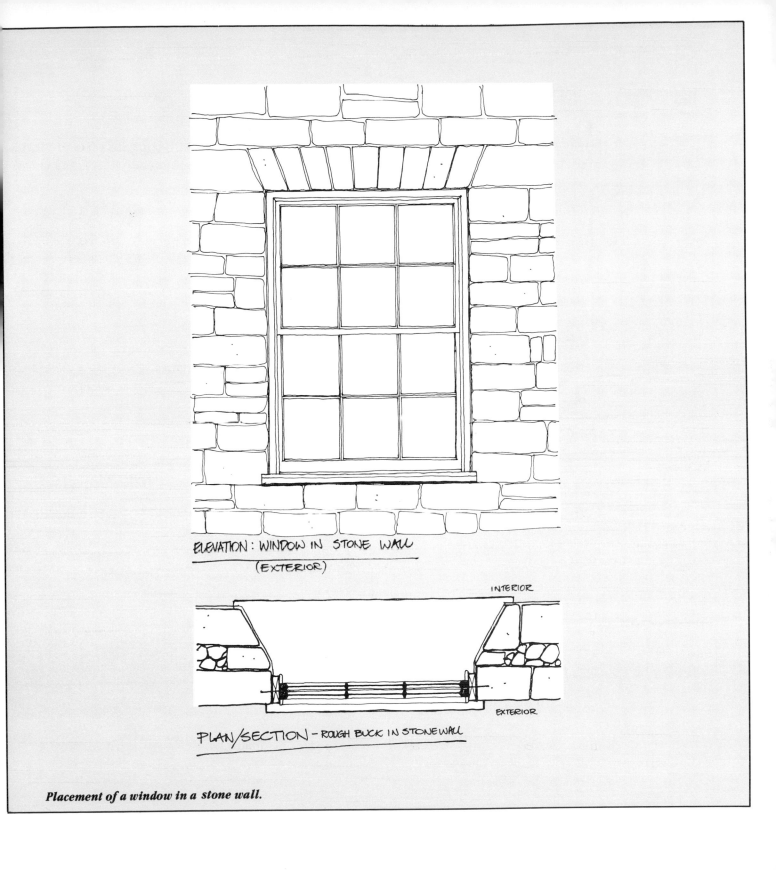

ELEVATION: WINDOW IN STONE WALL
(EXTERIOR)

INTERIOR

EXTERIOR

PLAN/SECTION - ROUGH BUCK IN STONE WALL

Placement of a window in a stone wall.

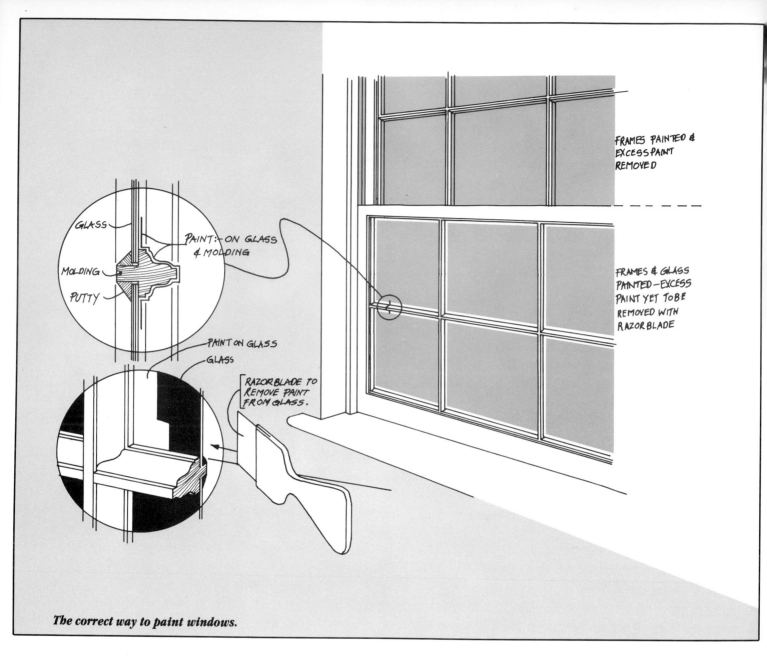

GLASS

PAINT: ON GLASS & MOLDING

MOLDING

PUTTY

PAINT ON GLASS

GLASS

RAZOR BLADE TO REMOVE PAINT FROM GLASS.

FRAMES PAINTED & EXCESS PAINT REMOVED

FRAMES & GLASS PAINTED — EXCESS PAINT YET TO BE REMOVED WITH RAZOR BLADE

The correct way to paint windows.

dow opening. Second, construct a rough frame or buck, coat it with preservative, and install it in the opening. The new window unit will come as a boxed-in assembly, with all the mechanisms (pulleys, sliders, etc.) contained in it. Third, position it in the rough buck and level it by using shims. Once it is firmly anchored in place, it may then be trimmed and painted. New window assemblies ordinarily come with a primer coat.

Whether you are repairing an original window or providing the glass for a whole new unit, the cost of glass has made that pile of storm windows in the basement a valuable commodity. Early Crown glass and later, more modern glass can both still be found and reasonably purchased at country auctions or the local junkyard. Sometimes, it is possible to

A classic Loyalist entranceway. Niagara-on-the-Lake, Ontario, 1820.

purchase entire units from wreckers or at the demolition site of an old building. These are only useful if they fit your window openings, but if you are planning an addition in the same style as the house, they can be a source of great savings.

DOORS

The entrance to the house and its surround, both in trim and glass, is the focal point of the front elevation—the area of use, the area of business, but also the area of style. Being a focal point brings with it the stress and fatigue suffered by those at the center of attention. Physical abuse, the scuffling of feet, the scratching of paws, the natural wearing away of door sills all prematurely age exterior doors. The effects of a warm interior and a cold exterior often lead to shrinking and distortion, both in plank doors and those with inset panels. As with the rest of the house, structural movement wreaks havoc upon a mechanism theoretically able only to function when level and square.

Remedies are relatively obvious, and yearly maintenance inspections should take place. Physical deterioration can frequently be corrected by the addition of new wood and the installation of kick plates. Adequate preservatives should be continually used and maintained. Where distortion or joint expansion has occurred, it may be possible in early panel doors (pre-1835) to drill out the pegs, reassemble, and reglue the entire unit.

In a restoration, door hardware should be of the period. Where rehabilitation is in order, a lock assembly of well-designed proportions may be used. In areas where winters are severe, a storm door is needed. A reproduction of the main door is recommended, although it is quite acceptable to use a door of lesser quality for a storm. Most Loyalist front doors, for example, were made in the Cross and Bible style, while the storm door was made of beaded planks. The use of aluminum doors in rehabilitations and restorations is most unacceptable.

While a recycled door of the period may be thoroughly workable on an addition where the frame can be built around it, it is virtually impossible to find a door to fit an opening not made for it. Exterior doors are a major source of heat loss and therefore must fit snugly. If a new door is required, many is the skilled craftsman who could reproduce a door not only architecturally complementary to the house, but one which would also protect you from the cold.

Worn sills may be part of the charm of an old house, but further deterioration invites insect and moisture damage.

This fine panel door has been altered to accommodate an uninspired window addition.

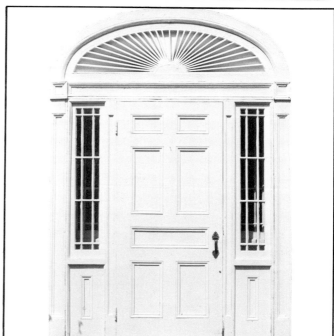

A storm door that has a screen for summer cooling and a wooden panel for winter protection. Ontario, 1825-1835.

A charming Loyalist door with a wooden transom fan rather than glass. Rideau Corridor, Ontario, 1825-1835.

A Cross and Bible door. Frankville, Ontario, pre-1835.

A Federalist-inspired door. Perth, Ontario, mid-nineteenth century.

Plank door. Limerick, Maine, last quarter eighteenth century.

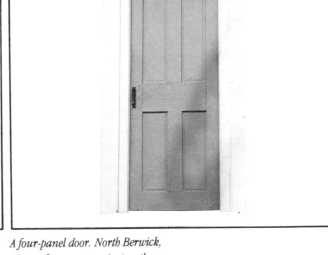

A four-panel door. North Berwick, Maine, first quarter nineteenth century.

A raised-panel door and period surround. North Berwick, Maine, third quarter eighteenth century.

A Federal entrance with ornate metal tracery. New England, circa 1820.

A double-panel door with shutters. Virginia, late 1700s.

ROOF

The roof is the hat of the house, its obvious role being protection from the weather. It is made up of three distinct elements. The support system or framework (rafters, trusses, etc.) provides its structural integrity. On top of this is some form of sheathing, usually planks, which gives lateral support to the rafters and forms the base for the third element, the cladding. As with other aspects of the house, the roof structure in North America has evolved from its European descendants. Where climate and materials dictated, roof styles were changed to suit a particular region.

The use of clapboard as roof cladding is perhaps an ideal example of this kind of vernacular adaptation. The Adam Thoroughgood House in Virginia Beach, Virginia, is clad with a feather-edged white oak clapboard, an obvious concession to the ready availability of oak in that area. In the 1600s, thatched roofs were initially used in North America as they were in Europe, but problems with differences in materials and the Indians' burning arrow soon put an end to their use. The earliest form of shanty was roofed with overlapping logs covered with moss, an expedient but hardly durable covering against the elements.

Throughout the late 1600s and early 1700s, slate roofs were being used in both the French settlements of early Quebec and the English settlements in Virginia and Pennsylvania. As early as 1728, slate was being quarried at Grand Etagne on Cape Breton's coast. In fact, slate was relatively common in New France. Melbourne, Quebec, was perhaps the largest slate quarry in Canada and is noted for supplying the slate for the roofing of Canada's first Parliament Building. Because slate was fireproof, durable, and flexible, it lent itself to the demands of the Victorian era. Charming multi-patterned roofs of slate dotted small town Canada during this period and are still a dominant feature of some small town skylines.

The locations of quarries capable of producing slate and their proximity to the construction sites were significant factors in the use of this material because of weight restrictions and obvious transportation problems. Other materials were pressed into service. Records in the Dutch settlement of New Utrecht, New York, document that by the late 1600s roofers employed red tile for cladding.[2] As mentioned in Chapter 5, brick was available in New Utrecht at approximately the same time as tile, and one might surmise that they came from the same kilns.

Wood shingles as roof cladding appeared early in North American settlement. Pine and cedar were commonly used, for they were long-lasting and easily workable. It is not unusual today, when reroofing, to find vestiges of the original wood shingles still in place under one or two layers of other materials.

The tinsmith's trade was not ignored in the roofing process. Tin raised batten, raised seam, and cross-hatched roofs all became popular by the 1840s. Their durability is evident in their usual excellent condition today; they may, in fact, only require some renailing.

During the mid-Victorian period, what we now know as asphalt roofing came into vogue. The process was imported from Europe, and its use was somewhat tempered on this side of the ocean, because the fall freeze-thaw cycle tended to leave

Basic rafters make up the framework for the roof sheathing of this house. Ontario, last quarter nineteenth century.

A complex truss system. Quebec, mid-1700s.

large cracks during winter months. By 1900, the early asphalt shingle had appeared. Quite flexible, it was made up of a combination of asphalt, fibrous pulp, and colored sand which was formed under pressure in machines. The light weight, flexibility, and low cost of the asphalt shingle, combined with the ease with which it could be nailed to planking, made it the cladding of the future.

Without a sound roof the rest of the structure is virtually left at the mercy of the elements. Throughout previous chapters moisture and the deterioration it causes have frequently been traced to such roofing problems as leaks, improper downspouts, and inadequate drainage. Either historical underdesign or the ravages of old age may cause the roof to be unable to deal with wind or snowloads. Here, major surgery is necessary, an expensive but

necessary procedure. A minor repair or patch job might uncover the magnitude of the devastation, and as often as not rafters need to be doubled up and collar ties added.

Time may simply have worn the roof out. Wood shingles have weathered away, flashing has rusted through or, even if the actual cladding is still in reasonable condition, the original ungalvinized fastenings have rusted away. The presence of moss and lichens, coupled with overfilled gutters, creates ideal conditions for the growth of fungi and the development of rot. It is quite likely that the roof has not been spared human abuse. The fact that most people are not particularly interested in heights, and roof repairs are often quite expensive, leads to poor patch jobs and unacceptable reroofing procedures. It is not uncommon to find a roof clad

Detail of a crimped-seam metal roof. Ontario, 1850-1900.

A slate roof. Quebec, early 1700s.

A standing seam metal roof, another good investment in roof cladding. Maine, nineteenth century.

Repair of roof cladding, such as these decorative tiles, in period materials is often cost prohibitive, and suitable alternatives must be found. Toronto, Ontario, circa 1880.

A plank roof on a French Regime building. Quebec, first half eighteenth century.

A raised batten roof is an excellent long-term investment in roof cladding. Quebec, nineteenth century.

in wood shingles, asphalt shingles, and then tin on top, perhaps the theory being the more roof the less moisture penetration.

Cladding failure will probably lead to structural failure of the support system. Rafter ends are often the first victims, because they sit on the edge of the building where ice build-up and gutter deficiencies may have caused undue amounts of moisture to enter. The problems inherent in a worn-out roof are accentuated by variables of climate. The oft mentioned freeze-thaw cycle has the same effect as a man with a pry bar. It is not hard to see how serious damage can be done in one mild winter.

As the availability of energy becomes a major problem in today's world, the use of it and subsequent adaptations for its use cause previously unforeseen dangers for the roof structure. Large amounts of insulation may be added to the garret (attic) without provision for proper ventilation, giving rise to yet another moisture problem – condensation. Structural damage can result if this condition is not rectified. Even if vapor barriers and insulation are properly installed, the new extreme barriers of hot and cold may create problems unknown in the previous history of the house.

Roof repairs are of paramount importance in flow chart planning. It is pointless to consider insulating, painting, and so on without a secure roof. As mentioned before, roof repairs are often costly. The people who buy a period home are no doubt looking for longevity and quality, and that is why they bought a house of the past in the first place. If the budget allows, the quality of traditional roofing materials has not been surpassed. Not only will such materials as slate and metal provide, in most cases, a lifetime of coverage (thirty-five to sixty years), but

they will also help restore the house to its original appearance. Just as the hat of the individual should complement the individual's taste and style, so too should the hat of the house portray the social station and condition of the structure. Just as fenestration highlights the exterior and provides stylistic themes, the design, cladding, and decorative treatment dress the roof.

Materials for reroofing or repairs should be examined for lifespan, wearability, and appearance. Combinations may be used. The asphalt shingle roof with metal on the edges is ideal where ice dams are prevalent. In order of cost, asphalt shingles win hands down. The neutral appearance of a black or grey color does nothing to detract from the period house. Such a roof is easily installed, available everywhere, and has a life expectancy of up to twenty-five years.

Wood shingles are practical in areas where they are available locally. Their cost and installation are marginally more than asphalt, but their appearance and longer life makes them desirable when historically correct. However, if building codes require the use of a fire retardant, the cost may double, and installation may make necessary such practices as soaking nails to pierce the now brittle shingles.

Tin is expensive, but substitute metals, sometimes with baked-on color, are a cheaper alternative. These can be quite costly, though, because they require skilled labor for the application. Prospective purchasers of metal roofs in traditional styles may find that this craft has died out in their area. When restoring an 1860 structure in a city a few years ago, architectural evidence was introduced to show that it had been clad with a raised batten tin roof, a method quite common in that area and

Wood shingles are still an economically feasible, long-wearing cladding.

Here plywood is being applied over the original planks to provide a smooth, even surface for wood or asphalt shingles.

A collage of deterioration symptoms. Improper maintenance invites serious problems. (A) Worn-out wood shingles. (B) Sheathing deterioration due to moisture and insect attack. (C) Initial insect infestation has led to further damage by animals. (D) and (E) Improper roof maintenance may result in extensive structural decay.

Repairing the cornice of an 1835 house in eastern Ontario. Period building techniques and style are carefully repeated, but the repaired eave is clad in painted aluminum bent to the original eave shape. This is a relatively maintenance-free alternative, which is in keeping with the period.

period. Requests were sent out to five roofers for cost estimates covering installation only (the metal would be provided). Each request also asked for a sample panel to be made up. The lowest bid came from a man from the country whose father had taught him the craft. His workmanship was excellent, using bends and sleeves rather than nails. Two other bidders with reasonably good work were next, and the fact that they were both from the city might have had something to do with their higher bids. The gentleman with the highest bid (one hundred and fifty per cent more than the first) was also distinguished by his unacceptable workmanship. The first man got the contract, not only because of price and quality, but because of his ready enthusiasm in being able to work again on what he called "a real roof."

Joints and edges are the most susceptible roof areas for decay. Flashings, usually strips of metal which exclude water from the junction of a roof covering and another surface, are subject to the usual freeze-thaw deterioration, vegetation attack, and maintenance problems. All too frequently workmen find it easier to climb the roof by running up the valleys, damaging flashings in the process. Flashings should be kept clear of junk build-up, and those around chimneys and stack pipes should have well-caulked joints, because they are havens for moisture. Finally, the color of all of them should be in harmony with the rest of the roof.

The most basic form of watershed or rafter overlap is called the eave. In its simplest form and without any guttering attached, it is not an area particularly prone to deterioration, apart from such physical abuse as being sawn off during the installation of some form of siding or broken by a tree planted too close to the house. As architectural style replaced simple utilitarianism, however, the eave evolved into the cornice. The cornice brought with it a certain amount of elegance and embellishment. It also brought difficulties in maintenance. Boxed-in eave returns were perfect places for squirrels and birds to nest. Ice build-up on the roof caused water to permeate the first two or three layers of shingle or tile, giving rise to wet rot. Gutters, already subject to ice attack, were easily blocked with leaves and branches causing still more wet rot. Some forms of the Neoclassical house had interior guttering. In one such Upper Canadian example, it is thought that it was never successful even from the day of its construction. The French Robertson house, Upper Canada Village, Morrisburg, Ontario, is dated 1820, and its guttering system has been inspected, and changes recommended, by more architects, engineers, and restoration technologists than any other in North America. It still leaks.

Even as late as the 1930s or 1940s, the cistern in the basement was the primary source of water for washing. Frequently, elaborate systems fed rainwater through a maze of pipes to this concrete or stone box. The individual leaning towards a more pure form of restoration might want to resurrect this system; it adds a fascinating domestic aspect to the mechanical workings of the house and provides a fairly pure form of soft water. In any case, be wary of systems that look all right. Starting from the roof, it may be possible to find moisture problems stemming from the path of the down-pipes.

Although water runoff is an ever-present problem, in areas of severe winter conditions the use of guttering has never been satisfactory. This is true of the plank gutters that were common until the Victo-

Judging from the patching along the base, inadequate roof drainage has been a problem for some time.

rian period and of the more ornate, mass-produced gutters available later. In almost all cases, whether original or restored, the weight of snow and ice renders the system useless within five years. Even merely allowing runoff may cause related water problems in the basement or foundation. Therefore, a more efficient method of controlled drainage has been designed, which is illustrated on page 78.

DORMERS AND SKYLIGHTS

In the discussion of windows, it was noted that the absence of light in early houses was cause for some concern. As a result, dormers were often added to bring in the sun. An interesting evolution of what is basically a large dormer is the appearance of the gable in eastern Ontario. Early settlement houses in

A luxury of the past, copper gutters are aesthetically pleasing and properly maintained, can last as long as a hundred years.

This 1880 brick house still had the cistern in the basement. Unfortunately, the in-flow pipe led the water in more detrimental directions.

Two delightful examples of eaves troughing. The finely detailed French Robertson house (circa 1830) in Upper Canada Village, Ontario, and an equally out-standing demonstration of the tinsmith's art, a rain collector box made in the mid-nineteenth century.

Chimney flashing needs regular maintenance checks to prevent water penetration.

Contemporary skylights, with their clean lines, combine well with Victorian houses.

This center gable with its window lets light into a previously dark upstairs hall. St. Andrews, New Brunswick, mid-nineteenth century.

An unobtrusive but practical skylight.

this area (1820-1830) were frequently straight one-and-a-half storey cottages. During the 1830s many of these houses had a center gable installed that either duplicated the symmetry of the downstairs opening or followed some other Georgian style. This let light into an otherwise pitch-dark upstairs hallway. As the century progressed, this gable became more severe, until by the 1870s the Gothic Revival style produced gable pitches of extreme proportions.

Today, the absence of light in the period home is no less a problem, especially considering the altered role the house will likely be fulfilling. Stylistically the addition of a dormer is frequently out of place. In fact, unless a massive shed dormer is installed, the amount of light admitted and space gained are negligible. The skylight, because of its design, adaptability, and cost, may be a desirable alternative.

PORCHES

Though the porch or verandah was probably born out of such extensions of the home as the lean-to shed attached to the saltbox house or the convenient breezeways connecting house to summer kitchen to drive shed, its function for the most part derives from Classical architectural forms. The verandah was relatively unknown before the 1800s in North America, despite the fact that it was soon to become an area of much practical and social use in the predominantly rural life of the past. By 1833, it had been documented in J. C. Louden's *Encyclopedia of Cottage, Farm and Villa Architecture and Furniture*. Published in 1850, A. J. Downing's *The Architecture of Country Houses* contained a design

for a symmetrical, bracketed cottage with a verandah. Downing described it as a

pretty little open porch, with its overhanging window and its seat, where, in the cooler hours of the day, the husband, the wife, and the children may sit and enjoy the fresh breath of morning or evening hours. . . .[3]

In many instances, the verandah was a later addition, and, like the summer kitchen, it was often built on a virtually nonexistent foundation. As gutterings break and the joints between porch, roof, and house fail, the verandah literally sinks into the ground. Hooks that may once have held the porch roof in place may rust out, leading to roof collapse. Deterioration from the elements gives rise to rot and insect attack. The human attitude in the past might have led to removal rather than repair.

Wherever possible, the original verandah should be restored to its rightful position as a legitimate part of the house. New footings can be easily and cheaply poured with the use of sonar tube containers. General repairs can be made *in situ* as money and time dictate. (Again, it is imperative to coat all new wood with a preservative.) As with the main roof, the cladding, sheathing, and flashings must be checked and maintained. Once the structure has been made sound, the porch must be looked after. Steps and areas of heavy traffic should be painted more often than little-used areas. Where the base and, in Victorian porches, trellis work are in close proximity to the ground and vegetation, care must be taken to prevent the development of wet rot. No wood should be in contact with the ground.

All too frequently the original verandah is badly mutilated and beyond repair. In this case, your research may be of great help if you have been able

A past lifestyle of leisure is probably indicated by the effort put into this grand verandah. Merrickville, Ontario, mid-nineteenth century.

*A delightful Gothic verandah.
Ontario, third quarter nineteenth
century.*

*A Richardson Romanesque veran-
dah in obvious need of treatment.
Toronto, Ontario 1880s.*

*This whimsical Victorian balcony
with a cast railing has been added
to an earlier New England house.*

A verandah of charm, eloquence and, unfortunately, some decay. Inadequate footings have resulted in settlement. The bowed posts were caused by inadequate drainage which allowed the post-ends to rot away. Temporary shoring has prevented further deterioration. Ontario, second quarter nineteenth century.

Historical photographs helped the preservationist of this Victorian house to restore the verandah. The original had been completely destroyed.

A rehabilitated complex of rowhouses in Ottawa, Ontario, 1900. New verandahs and decks have been designed to give both individuality and harmony to the block.

to obtain early sketches, prints, or photographs showing what the porch looked liked in earlier years. Steps for replacement are those of building a new structure: adequate footings should be poured, preservatives must coat all new woods. Most of all, the style must follow the original both in space usage and material texture.

CHAPTER SEVEN

Mechanical Systems

THE ADAPTATION OF MODERN MECHANICAL systems to fit the period house while meeting the physical, financial, and climatic needs of the owner is a process that requires careful thought and, inevitably, some compromise. The previous chapter has left the house enclosed in some form of weathertight condition. At this point the problem of mechanical installations must be examined. Structural rehabilitation (space usage) and historical rehabilitation may take two distinctly different paths. In space usage it is often possible and economical to leave the mechanical systems exposed, stating in their exposure that they themselves are design elements. It becomes evident in this process that the designer or architect is moving into the contemporary field of the interior decorator.

In the historical rehabilitation, and in the broad sphere between its demands and those of space usage, lie the many problems of marrying new mechanical elements to the period structure. It is imperative that heating, wiring, and plumbing needs be analyzed following the process outlined in Chapter 3. That is, there must be a balance between historical accuracy and the contemporary requirements of twentieth-century life.

HEATING AND INSULATION

The meshing of past and present is nowhere more problematic than in heating and insulation. Following the 1973 Arab oil crisis and subsequent energy supply problems, governments have begun to reassess the efficiency of fuel consumption in the individual home and to take steps to prevent waste. In this wave of reactionary measures, insulation pro-

grams have been introduced and the home-owner subsidized with grants. As admirable as these programs are, little attention has been paid to adequate venting. The result has been condensation problems, leading to wet rot, which affect both new-built and old structures. These problems are especially critical in the old house, because it was not originally constructed to be well sealed and heavily insulated. To correctly analyze the difficulties that new heating systems and insulation modes can cause, we must again return to the past. How was the house originally heated?

The early inhabitants of the eastern seaboard of North America settled an area whose vegetation was unlike what had existed in Europe for nearly two centuries. The major forests of Europe had been cut and not replenished. What wood was cut from remaining stands was used for such things as ornamental trim, not fuel. Peat and coal had replaced wood as the primary heat source. The primeval forests of North America must have seemed an endless supply of free fuel to the early settler.

The fireplace was the source of heat. Following English prototypes, large fireplaces were to be found downstairs, primarily for cooking, while smaller ones were used in the parlors and bedrooms of more substantial houses. Because of the romantic notion of happy settlers seated around the blazing kitchen fire, today we have come to regard the fireplace with a certain amount of colonial reverence. Due to the size of these original fireplaces and the fact that until the mid-1700s no form of damper was used in the flue, the fireplace was, in fact, a horrendously inefficient means of keeping warm. In spite of six- to ten-foot openings piled high with virgin maple and other such heat-producing hardwoods, the majority of the heat would go up the flue. Ten per cent efficiency would not be an exaggerated ratio. Not only were they inefficient, they were also dangerous; their shape and continual use made fire an ever-present hazard. In 1832, J. W. D. Moodie, husband of the author of *Roughing It in the Bush*, was moved to compose a poem on the value of such fireplaces:

Oh, the cold of Canada nobody knows,
The fire burns our shoes without warming our toes;
Oh, dear, what shall we do?
Our blankets are thin, and our noses are blue —
Our noses are blue, and our blankets are thin,
It's at zero without, and we're freezing within![1]

Peter Kalm, in his *Travels in North America* (1812), observed that "an incredible amount of wood is squandered in this country for fuel; day and night all winter, or for nearly half the year, in all rooms, a fire is kept going."[2] By the mid-1700s, the amount of fuel used in operating colonial fireplaces was causing some alarm, and shortages were noted as early as 1770. Apart from flying kites, Benjamin Franklin also designed a more efficient stove-fireplace combination. This was to become the foundation of what we now know as the Franklin Fireplace. Franklin was neither first nor alone. A form of tile stove had been developed in fourteenth-century Germany, and by the late 1700s Germanic settlements in North America were involved in stove manufacturing. Moravian potters in North Carolina were producing a tile stove of relatively sophisticated design by 1800. In the 1700s stove manufacturing was not limited to the Thirteen Colonies. The Forge du St. Maurice near Trois Rivières, Quebec, produced stoves from at

An early form of ductwork took the form of stovepipe running all through the house.

When the kitchen was partitioned into parlor and bedroom, heat transfer holes (behind the door to the right of the chair in this photograph) were often included — a crude but effective form of central heating. Upper Canada Village, Morrisburg, Ontario, 1820.

The burnt-out shell of this stone house reveals chimney runs and both fireplace and wood stove outlet holes.

The charm of this early fireplace (Maine, last quarter eighteenth century) is not matched by its efficiency as a heat source. Not until Count Rumford's 1791 treatise did any form of fireplace efficiency come into being.

The cast iron fireplace inset was only one of Benjamin Franklin's contributions to heating technology. North Berwick, Maine, 1800.

The Franklin stove. King's Landing, New Brunswick, 1800.

No wonder the family moved to the summer kitchen in warmer weather.

least 1752 on.[3] Many of these early box stoves have been discovered in early settlements along the St. Lawrence River.

Advertisements for St. Maurice stoves pointed out that they were superior to the Scottish stoves then being imported, because the metal used was pliable and durable with no cracking problems. These claims must have been an early adman's dream. From the beginning St. Maurice stoves suffered from poor quality materials. The history of the forge is dotted with bankruptcies, and although historically of some note, the merchandise was less than excellent.

By 1830, cooking and heating stoves had come into general use, spurred on in Ontario by a government tax on fireplaces.[4] The changeover from fireplace to stove made it easier on the family cook and provided more efficient heating and fuel consumption. Gas began to be employed by the mid-nineteenth century and, along with coal, it was the main source of heating until oil and electricity were economically available.

Heating systems can be broken down into a variety of categories; any one or any combination can be chosen by the preservationist. They are: original source (fireplaces, wood stoves), electric baseboard heating, oil furnace, natural gas, steam, wood and oil, and solar.

It should be kept in mind from the outset that the original heating system of the pre-1850 house is only for the purest of purists. This is not to say that in combination with another, back-up form of heating it may not be successful and perhaps the most effective system for the period structure. Any system must be analyzed for availability, initial cost, long-term cost effectiveness, and the impact on the house in both mechanical and aesthetic terms. Being a personal advocate of wood-stove heating, it may be of interest to note the cost differential between wood and other forms of heat. It has been my experience that for every thirty-five dollars spent on wood one hundred and sixty would go to other heating forms (one cord of wood = two hundred gallons of oil = four thousand kilowatt hours = one ton of coal).

Early houses, whether stone, brick, or wood frame, all contained freshly cut timber. For the most part, this timber was not allowed to dry adequately. The settlers were fighting the elements, unfriendly Indians, and natural disasters, and they did not have the luxury of time to allow the wood to season. The house would usually be completed in summer or fall, and the family moved in immediately. Neither the fireplace nor the later stove was particularly efficient, and insulation, if any, was of rudimentary quality, so the structure was never subjected to extremes of heat or cold. Once the period structure has been basically insulated and a forced-air system installed, a drying-out process will take place within the first two or three months of the first winter; this process is unlike anything previously experienced in the history of the house. Whereas in the previous two hundred years heating and cooling were gradual processes, extremes are now introduced causing undue stress on all elements from the framework to the fastenings. Nails popping out of plaster lath is a tell-tale sign.

One example that illustrates this process is the antique collector who buys from a country auction. Often the house from which the piece comes is inadequately heated in contemporary terms. The moisture content of the piece is, say, ten per cent. When it is moved to a dry seventy-two degree

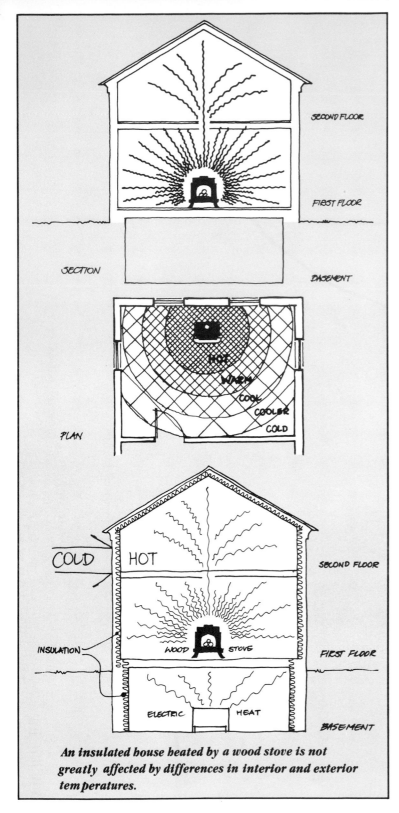

SECTION

SECOND FLOOR

FIRST FLOOR

BASEMENT

PLAN

HOT

WARM

COOL

COOLER

COLD

COLD   HOT

INSULATION

WOOD   STOVE

ELECTRIC   HEAT

SECOND FLOOR

FIRST FLOOR

BASEMENT

An insulated house heated by a wood stove is not greatly affected by differences in interior and exterior temperatures.

climate, its moisture content may drop very rapidly to two per cent, causing cracking or shrinkage. Another instance is the person installing large amounts of woodwork in a new house. Even though Grade One wood is being used, the moisture content will drop considerably, resulting in the same cupping, warping, and shrinking experienced by the antique collector. When examining these minor examples, it is not hard to see the damage that can be done to the period structure by a warm, dry atmosphere.

Apart from the work and the shivering involved, the original heat sources used were ideal. Basically, there are three types of heat movement. The first is conduction which might be illustrated by putting a pan on a stove; when you grasp the handle it is hot because heat has been conducted to it. The second is convection, the transfer of heat by another agent, usually air. When air is heated, it rises, forming convection currents. Radiation, on the other hand, transmits heat in waves, the same as light. Both the wood stove and the fireplace emitted radiant heat and convection currents let it rise, in turn heating upstairs rooms. If one can emulate this form of heating, but on a more sophisticated level by combining a new heat source with insulation and storm windows, a satisfactory system can be accomplished. On the whole, electric baseboard heating without extremely good insulation is neither effective nor cost-effective in the period home. However, if the house is to be gutted (reduced to a shell) and insulated to today's standards, then its effectiveness and ready availability make it a good long-term investment.

A good compromise can be reached by using baseboard heaters as a back-up system to a wood-

Ductwork leading to the second floor is being installed in a stud wall. The wiring runs follow a similar path to minimize disturbance of the original plasterwork.

This brick addition of the late 1800s has not fared well with contemporary heating systems. Heat loss and the lack of a vapor barrier have led to deterioration of the outer wall through moisture build-up.

This forced-air vent has been well masked.

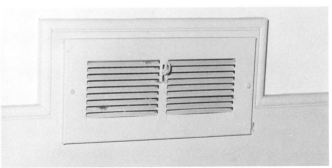

Electric blower units are effective in areas such as summer kitchens where small crawl spaces are the norm.

Radiators in various styles not only add period technological detail, but are also an extremely effective method of heating the older home.

The original heat source must frequently be replaced by one using less expensive fuel, such as natural gas.

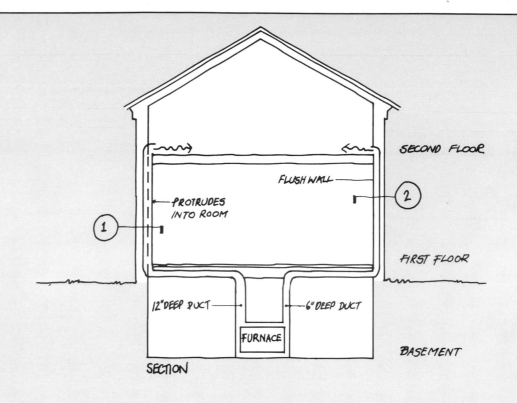

SECOND FLOOR

FLUSH WALL

②

PROTRUDES INTO ROOM

①

FIRST FLOOR

12" DEEP DUCT

6" DEEP DUCT

FURNACE

BASEMENT

SECTION

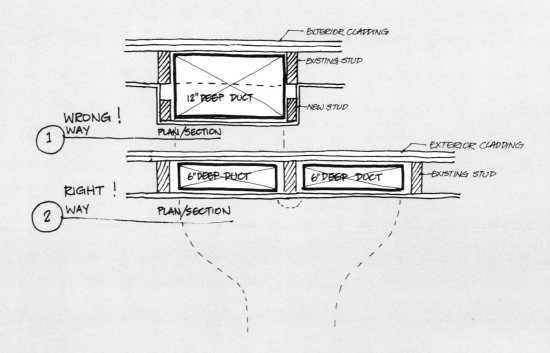

EXTERIOR CLADDING

EXISTING STUD

12" DEEP DUCT

NEW STUD

WRONG! WAY

①

PLAN/SECTION

EXTERIOR CLADDING

6" DEEP DUCT

6" DEEP DUCT

EXISTING STUD

RIGHT! WAY

②

PLAN/SECTION

Splitting the size of heating ducts reduces the disturbance of wall profiles and partitions.

A Victorian fireplace, last quarter nineteenth century. Note the fire-box size compared to the mantel.

burning device. Generally speaking, units can be installed without upsetting period features, and they can be painted to match trim.

Forced air heat, powered by oil, oil and wood, wood, gas, or electricity, is an even better system for the period house. By means of a blower, it pushes hot air through the house, giving overall warmth and comfort. In-line humidifiers can also keep the interior moisture level at an acceptable figure. On the premise that heat rises, it is often possible in smaller houses to duct downstairs liberally, with only one or two runs upstairs. Carlow Lodge, a Colonial Revival house in Burritt's Rapids, Ontario, functions well on this system. With approximately twenty-eight hundred square feet of living space, there are only two runs upstairs. The house has two fireplaces and adequate, but not excessive, insulation. The house is comfortable and, for its size, economical to operate.

The major problems with forced air systems are the availability of an economical fuel supply and the introduction of large ducting systems throughout the house. In many cases, it is easy to mask these ducts by splitting them and running them between wall studs. As often as not, however, early plastering details, complex baseboards, and panels are destroyed in their installation.

Historically, ductwork is not a new phenomenon. As stoves were more commonly used for heating, large systems of exposed piping ran all through the house. From the stove these pipes may have risen, turned ninety degrees and travelled through another room and a half before reaching a chimney. The ducts were put up in the fall and disassembled in the spring, with minor dismantling in-between for cleaning. The many duct sleeves found in floors

and walls bear witness to the popularity of this heating mode. These systems were relatively effective, and it is unfortunate that virtually no one uses them today.

Victorian and Edwardian houses, as well as earlier structures rehabilitated in the first half of this century, are often equipped with steam heat. Although out of favor for most of the century, steam heat is reappearing as one of the "new" energy alternatives. Basically, steam heating is made up of a heating plant (burner and boiler) and a distribution system linked to radiators, the source of radiant heat. Because of the extremely durable materials used in the construction of these early systems, all that may be required is a maintenance overhaul to make them function efficiently. Of course, changing fuel availability may make it necessary to replace the original heat plant.

A parlor fireplace. New England, third quarter eighteenth century.

The inefficient large fireplace gave way to the stove by the early 1800s. In this example, the firebox has been filled in and a stove hole cut in the flue.

An Adamesque mantel and fire-board. Ontario, second quarter nineteenth century.

In this historical rehabilitation, the style of the reproduction mantel was based on local research. Ontario, first quarter nineteenth century.

A contemporary fireplace built on Rumford's principles in a new addition to a period house.

Years of use have worn out the mortar in this firebox, resulting in loose stones. It should be rebuilt using correct period materials and tooling methods.

Front and rear views of a firebox. The brick is corbelling (projecting).

The system should be drained and flushed to remove loose particles built up over the years. House settlement or alterations may have left floors and radiators out of square. These should be leveled. Valves, gaskets, and washers should be checked for tightness. Valves or nuts should be left either on or off, never halfway. Steam heat has advantages. The major installation is already complete, it is often in keeping with the period of the structure and it gives an overall, low-level radiant heat. On the minus side, steam heat is extremely dry, and it will probably be necessary to use humidifiers.

The romance of the fireplace is frequently an important part of the would-be preservationist's vision of the old house. In my experiences with clients, a fireplace is always included in the first draft of any rehabilitation scheme. Its magic lure is well emphasized by the fact that in spite of cost and dubious efficiency it usually remains where a much cheaper, more efficient, and historically correct parlor stove would have sufficed. Large early fireplaces were either built on a substantial base or, as in some New England forms, on a vaulted support. This support was open in the middle and became a kind of closet affair reputedly used to hide slaves. More often than not, though, it was used as a smoke cellar.

The center chimneys of early New England houses carried in them flues for all the fireplaces. They were constructed of the same materials used in the rest of the structure. An interesting footnote in the history of available materials is the pargeting technique used in the interiors of some of these chimneys; they were coated with a mixture of mortar and cow dung.

Earlier chimney forms were built using sticks and clay. As they are renowned for their combustibility,

we will dwell no longer on them.

Discovering a fireplace hidden in a plastered-over wall can be an exciting experience. Obvious clues may be foundations with hearthstones underneath the floor, patches in floors where hearths have been removed, a comparison of the use of stoves in your area with the age of the house and, in the case of log houses, a stone or brick rectangle at the base of a gable end (the back of the fireplace).

Keeping the flue clean is of paramount importance. Even though one may follow sound principles of wood heating, using seasoned, year-old hardwood, creosote deposits will occur. This is particularly true in the top part of the chimney, where creosote cools quickly and condensation is more likely to happen. Caked creosote will ignite. Chimneys should be cleaned yearly with a fireplace and more frequently with a period stove or one of the new airtight types.

When restoring the period fireplace and chimney, earlier methods of construction are worth duplicating. Flues should be checked for blockage by such things as birds' nests. The use of a smoke bomb or moist leaves on a low fire will point out flue leaks. In some cases, the flue runs from basement to roof and it may have become an ideal passage for lazy tradesmen to run piping or wiring. As mentioned earlier, fireplaces were taxed from an early date in Ontario, and the degree to which people reacted to this regulation may be seen in the number of early chimneys that we can only assume were purposely pushed down the flue.

Problems in the firebox itself, both from the use of inferior materials like salmon brick and the obvious deterioration caused by many years of intense and continuous heat, may have worn away portions of the firebox walls or the hearth. These can easily

Three fireplaces in a similar style. New England, third quarter eighteenth century (left). Ontario, first quarter nineteenth century (right). Ontario, first quarter nineteenth century (below).

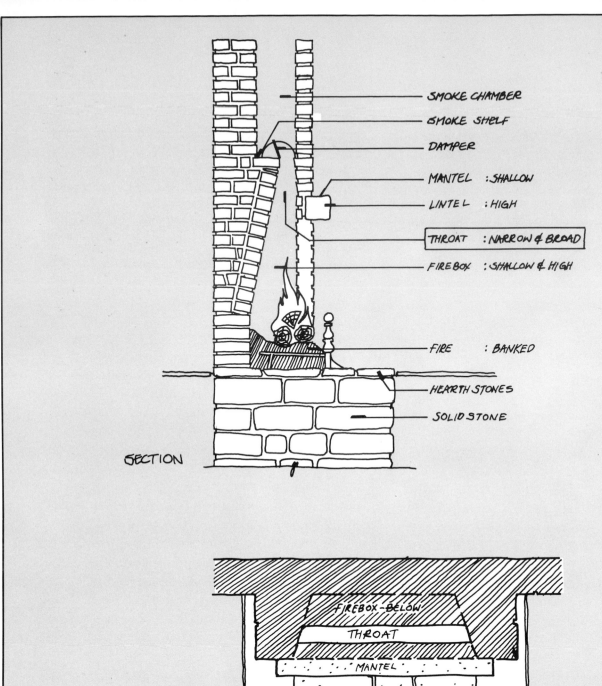

SMOKE CHAMBER

SMOKE SHELF

DAMPER

MANTEL   : SHALLOW

LINTEL   : HIGH

THROAT   : NARROW & BROAD

FIREBOX : SHALLOW & HIGH

FIRE   : BANKED

HEARTH STONES

SOLID STONE

SECTION

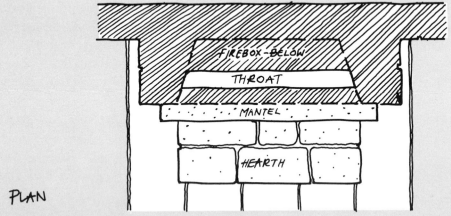

FIREBOX - BELOW

THROAT

MANTEL

HEARTH

PLAN

The Rumford fireplace.

be repaired by using similar construction methods and first-class materials. Fireplace hardware, such as dogs for the crane, should also be checked for deterioration and tested for stability. It is worth noting that the original firebox may have been built with incorrect proportions, causing undue smoking and poor drawing. In his 1796 essay on fireplaces,[5] the inventor and statesman Count Rumford set out the basic principles of firebox and chimney construction. Rumford knew that the fireplace primarily produced radiant heat. His ideal design was a tall, shallow firebox with the back and sides angled for maximum radiation. Even though his principles remain today the ultimate in fireplace design, contemporary masons are often quite ignorant of them. The result is the widespread belief that all fireplaces are grossly inefficient.

When building a new fireplace it is wise to follow Rumford's principles. A secure foundation must be constructed and the firebox built on it. A damper can be installed next and new flue tile used in the chimney. If insulation and heating standards are brought up to contemporary levels, it is often advisable to create a duct leading from the outside to the side wall of the firebox. Large fireplaces draw an amazing amount of air. When the house was not as well sealed, air seepage from outside walls was a natural phenomenon. Today's insulation, storm windows, and caulking can result in an airtight structure and poor fires.

Troublesome as it may be, large fireplace openings must have a damper installed. Ordinarily this is a custom operation. The throat, just before the smoke shelf, should be measured and a metal bracket constructed to fit, which should be lag-bolted and mortared into position. Some form of hinged assembly should then be tied into it. This is a two-piece job, the bracket and the actual damper. The space into which the assembly fits is usually very difficult to work in, and whatever areas of convenience are found should be used. Once the damper is in place, a handle can be attached, coming down to just above the fireplace lintel, convenient but out of sight. Pulleys or chains always clog with time, and a basic lever is advised.

If the flue is to be cleaned out by breaking through upstairs walls to get at an area unreachable from the roof or the firebox, it is possible to install a damper at this height, but difficulties in maintenance and chimney cleaning are obvious drawbacks.

Modes of heating must be examined with local climatic conditions in mind. What ideally may be referred to as alternate energy or passive solar heating may in fact be just common sense tips on how to operate the house more effectively. Advantage should be taken of surrounding mature vegetation in relation to the sun. Such devices as shutters, shades, drapes, and window awnings work most effectively in both shielding and retaining the sun's rays. Fans and blowers can be installed to economically move warm air around the house. Exterior paint colors are important in retaining and reflecting the sun's rays; dark colors absorb heat. Keeping thermostats turned down and dressing a little warmer are small prices to pay for energy economy.

Historically, the concept of insulation was almost unknown, although brick-noggin and rubble-stone infill were thought in the past to be significant in heat retention. On a minor scale, a mixture of sawdust and lime has been documented in frame structures and attics during the nineteenth century. One house of considerable historical importance, located in Lancaster, Ontario, was built in 1780 and insulated with earth. When a forced-air system was introduced three years ago, the condensation that was caused by lack of proper venting resulted in previously unforeseen problems. Mud trickled down the walls and through the ceiling. More often than not, the only insulation consisted of rags stuffed into major cracks plastered over with ten to twenty layers of wallpaper.

Before discussing the installation of major contemporary insulating products, it would be as well to go through a checklist of heat loss areas. Heat rises, and it is obvious that the roof is the single most susceptible place for heat to escape – twenty-five to forty per cent in the overall structure. Basements and crawl spaces run a close second, with windows and doors coming next.

The detailing of interior woodwork is of great importance in the atmosphere of the period home. For this reason I am personally loathe to disturb these elements, concentrating insulation efforts on the attic and basement, adding storm windows, caulking all construction joints, weatherstripping doors and windows, and generally sealing the house as well as possible. Single thickness window glass offers little protection from heat loss. Storm windows can rectify this problem to a large extent. For the double-hung window with a series of lights, it is more economical to use a storm with one bar in the center. Period detailing is not lost, and the storm is relatively cheap to produce. Thermopane units for large Victorian houses are easily designed to fit window openings. Aluminum (perish the thought) has reared its not always aesthetic, but often economically feasible head. If aluminum windows are

to be used, color co-ordinate them with the rest of the trim. Make sure the crossbars match up with the inside sash. Their availability, relative freedom from maintenance, and low cost make aluminum windows a recommended first step in storm window protection, but don't let the process end there.

In a house that requires extensive replastering, there is a method of creating a tighter interior space. The relief of most period mouldings is large enough to accept three-eighth inch drywall. The combination of drywall and the original plaster is very heat retentive. Drywall has the added benefits of being cheap and providing a fresh surface for paint or wallpaper. It can easily be removed if replastering is desired at a later date.

Insulation blocks the loss of heat due to the three processes of heat transfer: conduction, convection, and radiation. It is measured in R values (thermo resistance values). Contemporary insulation comes in three major types. Fiberglass batts are the most commonly used, are readily available, and economical. They can be fitted between studs, easily laid in attics and ceilings, or wrapped around duct work. Poured or blown insulation, made of mica, cellulose, or fiberglass wool, can be blown into attic spaces or wall cavities. Holes are drilled in outside walls, but these can be filled with wood plugs and painted out. Foam plastics are the newest, probably the most controversial, and certainly the most expensive form of insulation. The most commonly seen form of this last type are styrofoam sheets. These sheets have high R values, and their use in level, straight basement walls cannot be surpassed. They can also be effectively used in the recycled structure where interior roof structures are to be left exposed. The only drawback is that the sheets

A charming, late 1700s New England cape house. Contemporary passive solar units and a traditional wood stove are used as heat sources.

cannot be bent or twisted to fit particular areas. In the event of fire, the material gives off toxic fumes.

The newest kinds of foamed-in plastics are urea-formaldehyde resins. These are used in hard-to-reach wall cavities and attics. They can also be sprayed onto irregular surfaces, such as rubble-stone basement walls. Problems have arisen in the installation and long-term value of these resins. Cases have been recorded where the resins did not set up properly, oozing out onto floors with obvious results. On the other hand, they have also set up too quickly, popping nails in lath that was already fragile with age. This method was used in a Cobourg, Ontario, house and the material shrank drastically over a period of one and a half years. Toxic fumes can also be given off by these resins, both during installation and in the event of fire.

This review of resins might sound overly negative, but the point is that the introduction of new materials into the period home must be done with skill and care. Technically, the first two insulation types are more within the layman's grasp.

Exterior walls should be insulated last. Cellulose should be used in the attic once a vapor barrier is laid down on upstairs ceilings. Insulate basements with styrofoam sheets. Fiberglass batts are recommended for walls instead of blown insulation. Cavities in walls of any age are almost always filled with the nests of mice, squirrels, rats, or bats. Further blockage may be the result of wiring run through the walls. Insulation blown into the cavities will frequently go no further than the obstruction, leaving large, non-insulated voids.

When insulating walls, two things should be kept

Passive solar panels and a solar hot water unit blend well with this early nineteenth-century structure in New England.

Fortunately for the energy-conscious preservationist, dark colors were often used on the period house. Searsport, Maine, mid-1700s.

Sawdust or hay packed around the foundation for insulation in winter is still a common sight in rural areas.

Brick-noggin infill was presumed to have heat-retentive qualities; a theory with some validity. Upper Canada Village, Morrisburg, Ontario, first half nineteenth century.

in mind: the expense of the process and its effectiveness. If you are left with uninsulated voids, government grant or not, the money has been wasted. Therefore, if you are going to do it, make sure you do it properly. Be certain to follow proper documentation procedures (see Chapter 3) when gutting and reframing for batt insulation.

Condensation occurs in cold weather. Warm air hits cold air and moisture develops on the first hard surface nearby. The obvious result is wet rot. Vapor barriers should always be placed on the warm side of insulation (the side facing the heat source). In cases where blown insulation is used, and no vapor barrier can be applied, two coats of aluminum primer will serve the same function.

When adapting new mechanical systems to the period house it is imperative to examine potential condensation areas. All electric plugs, fans, etc., should be caulked to prevent heat loss and the collision of hot and cold air. Contemporary kitchens, bathrooms, and laundries expel large amounts of water vapor. This is not a problem in a house full of air leaks, but in a tightly sealed structure it can cause wet rot. Venting in the attic is of paramount importance. Dead air space in eaves and cornices is a perfect host for condensation and rot. The winter temperature in the attic should be within three degrees of that outside the house.

WIRING

Rewiring within an existing structure is time-consuming and problematic. It is therefore proportionately more expensive than wiring the newly

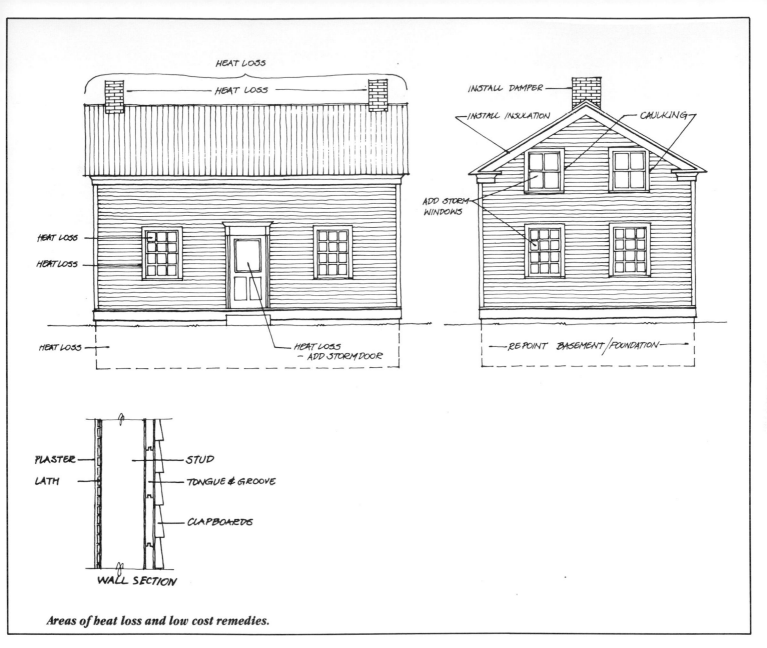

Areas of heat loss and low cost remedies.

framed house. It becomes, in fact, a technical design exercise, as well as a challenge in successful mechanical fitting. Any past wiring should be inspected for condition and total voltage. From the panel onwards, many older systems are not large enough for today's demands (electric heating or otherwise). Any new system should be started at the pole closest to the house. An underground system should be used, so as not to detract from the exterior appearance of the house. The cost for underground service in many cases may be no greater, and it has a much cleaner appearance, apart from the insistence of most hydro companies that the meter be put in an obvious place. Before rewiring, a detailed plan of your physical needs must be worked out. Most building codes will specifically

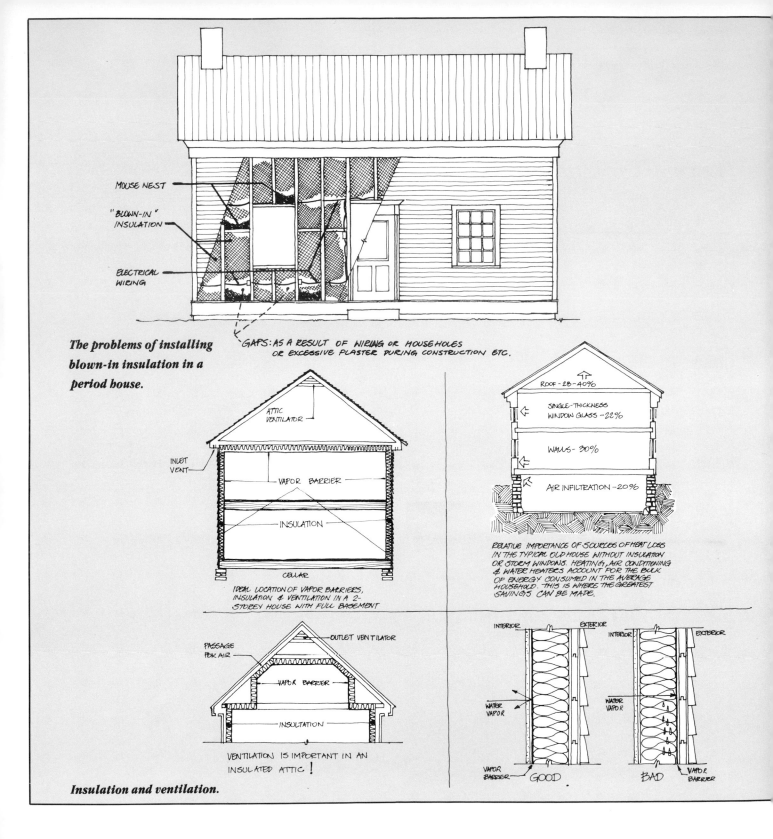

MOUSE NEST

"BLOWN-IN" INSULATION

ELECTRICAL WIRING

The problems of installing blown-in insulation in a period house.

GAPS: AS A RESULT OF WIRING OR MOUSEHOLES OR EXCESSIVE PLASTER DURING CONSTRUCTION ETC.

ATTIC VENTILATOR

INLET VENT

VAPOR BARRIER

INSULATION

CELLAR

IDEAL LOCATION OF VAPOR BARRIERS, INSULATION & VENTILATION IN A 2-STOREY HOUSE WITH FULL BASEMENT

ROOF - 28-40%

SINGLE-THICKNESS WINDOW GLASS - 22%

WALLS - 30%

AIR INFILTRATION - 20%

RELATIVE IMPORTANCE OF SOURCES OF HEAT LOSS IN THE TYPICAL OLD HOUSE WITHOUT INSULATION OR STORM WINDOWS. HEATING, AIR CONDITIONING & WATER HEATERS ACCOUNT FOR THE BULK OF ENERGY CONSUMED IN THE AVERAGE HOUSEHOLD. THIS IS WHERE THE GREATEST SAVINGS CAN BE MADE.

PASSAGE FOR AIR

OUTLET VENTILATOR

VAPOR BARRIER

INSULATION

VENTILATION IS IMPORTANT IN AN INSULATED ATTIC !

INTERIOR   EXTERIOR   INTERIOR   EXTERIOR

WATER VAPOR   WATER VAPOR

VAPOR BARRIER   GOOD   BAD   VAPOR BARRIER

Insulation and ventilation.

Reframe a period stone house as in new construction, but remember to keep as near to the original proportions as possible.

These basement walls have been insulated with rigid styrofoam.

Window wells are always a problem in a masonry structure. Not enough space exists between the woodwork and the stone to allow adequate insulation. Extensive caulking and rigid foam are usually the best solutions.

Rigid styrofoam has been used on the ceiling of this New England frame house. The framing has been left exposed as a design element, and also so the bed would fit. Limerick, Maine, last quarter eighteenth century.

Insulation between framing with vapor barrier attached.

Foam plastic insulation tends to shrink rendering it less than efficient.

A stone house with rigid insulation, vapor barrier, and drywall.

outline the wiring requirements for each room. It is important at this time to visually ascertain the positions of plugs, heaters, washing machines, and so on. Exterior electrical fittings, such as lighting and car plug-ins, should not be forgotten.

As mentioned in our discussion of windows in Chapter 6, light and the lack of it was an ever-present problem in the period house. Animal fats were used for fuel in early lighting devices. The making of tallow and wax candles was a definite improvement. Oil lamps were the prevalent lighting source in the individual home between 1800 and 1845, and between these dates more than five hundred patents on whale oil lamps alone were granted in North America. By the later 1800s, various forms of commercial gas lighting, which were based on William Murdock's gas distribution system devel-

oped in 1800 in England, were coming into vogue. On October 21, 1879, Thomas Edison burned an incandescent electric light bulb for forty hours, and by 1882 New York City was serviced by a rudimentary direct current system, although the use of gas lingered on until the 1920s.

In a historical rehabilitation, it is important to capture the mood of the period. Low-key lighting, for the most part, should be employed. Using the same basic method discussed under heating systems, original light sources should be analyzed and married to contemporary requirements. All too often, the impeccably rehabilitated 1830 house has its mood destroyed by glaring overhead lights. Space usage, on the other hand, may make use of various forms of clean, well-designed contemporary fixtures. Track lighting is a good example. In both

*Check with your electrician to find
the most easily accessible areas for
wiring runs.*

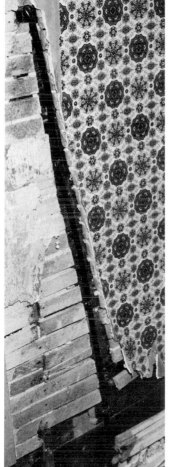

*An effective and reasonably priced
method of installing outlets in
older structures is this track wiring
with its movable plugs.*

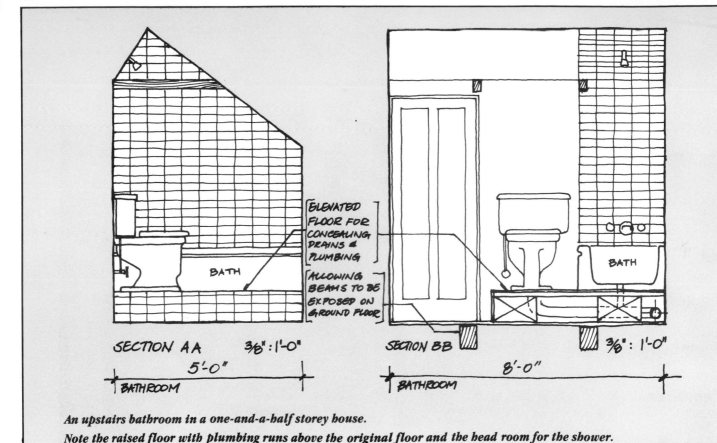

An upstairs bathroom in a one-and-a-half storey house.
Note the raised floor with plumbing runs above the original floor and the head room for the shower.

types of rehabilitation, switch and fixture locations must be well thought out in advance.

To prevent needless expenditures, care should be exercised during the rewiring process. In the rehabilitation of one 1860 log house, the electricians, tradesmen of excellent quality, were noticed installing wall plugs approximately two and a half feet off the floor. When asked why (it was assumed plugs would be placed in the baseboards), they replied that most people "don't like to bend over." Although a very complete plan had been worked out beforehand, this detail had been overlooked, certain rewiring had to take place, and costs were increased.

When the electrician arrives at the house for his initial inspection, slowly walk around the building explaining your requirements. Both of you must take the time to thoroughly discuss what is important to you about this house. Period details can easily be lost by being nonchalant about the placement of fixtures, plugs, and switches. Be specific. Once the electrician is familiar with the structure, ask him what would be easiest for him. More than likely he will have to fish wires through partitions and ceilings, often in cramped and difficult conditions. Compromise where necessary. You will save money, and he will take added interest in his work.

PLUMBING

The plumbing we now take for granted has a somewhat unique history in the march of technological evolution. In western civilization, the Romans were one of the first peoples to herald the idea of a

A sink in the mud-room is a necessity for country living.

Plumbing in the old house. (A) If the beams are to be exposed on the first floor, you may be forced to box bath and toilet returns. (B) Poor planning may result in the rerouting of pipes or the installation of a false ceiling to conceal them. (C) Plumbing runs should be parallel to floor joists. (D) This bathroom was installed in a one-and-a-half storey cape house. Note the angled door on the linen closet and the vent fan.

B

C

A

D

healthy mind in a healthy body, and in following this philosophy developed relatively sophisticated aqueduct and heating systems for their bath houses. The sacking of Rome in 476 A.D. effectively erased Roman innovations, and real improvements on their plans were not made until many centuries later. The general distribution of what we know as plumbing had to wait until the mid-nineteenth century.

Although Sir John Harrington developed a design for a flushing water closet during the reign of Elizabeth I, it was not until 1779 that John Bramah patented a hydraulic system, and not until the late 1860s on do we find advertisements for plumbing materials becoming commonplace. By 1870, George Jennings was specializing in the design of sanitary appliances; one of his New York advertisements offered

a patent tip up lavatory, and iron trap water closet and a large stock of plumber's materials, all of which are novelties and specialties, having the specific object of preventing the rising of sewer gas into dwellings [6]

Before the water closet came into vogue, the populace on the whole practised no sanitary habits. In the past, people might use the outdoor "jakes" or urinate in the corners of rooms. The large overhangs on Elizabethan houses were perhaps in part to provide shelter for passersby from the dumping of night soil out the windows. Chamberpots, commode chairs, and outhouses were all part of the evolution of today's toilet.

Washing, even in 1860, was thought to be something to do only occasionally for one's health. Rainwater was collected and harsh soap was produced domestically, both for the laundry and personal washing. The making of soft soap was quite an oper-

ation. Lye was leached out of ashes and to it was added all the bones and fat saved over the winter. When the lye had eaten as many bones and as much fat as it could, what remained was a liverlike soap. This was extremely powerful, and there is little wonder that washing was only a sometime thing.

Portable tubs were used, both for the laundry and more refined ones (zinc with mahogany trim) for bathing. The romantic image of the perfumed, aristocratic colonial gentleman decked out in wig, makeup, and heavily brocaded clothes is somewhat obscured by the fact that most of this was intended to mask the appalling stench of the person in question. By 1910, a cast-iron bathtub was commercially available at a reasonable price. Mass-production and technological advances led to the widespread use of the bathroom as we know it by the end of the First World War.

The contemporary bathroom is made up of a water source and a holding tank combined with a waste removal system. A thorough site inspection with the plumber is necessary. In urban areas tie-ins to water mains and sewage pipes will be co-ordinated through a city inspector. In the country, wells must be dug and septic tanks constructed. An undersized lot may demand the use of an aquarobic waste disposal system, which requires far less weeping tile than a septic tank.

As in the section on wiring, you must analyze the house for your needs. Kitchens, bathrooms, and laundry areas must be positioned according to physical requirements but also according to the compatibility of plumbing runs with the existing structure. Bear in mind that most people today require one and a half bathrooms.

Any new physical requirements, as discussed in Chapter 3, must be thoroughly thought out. In rural areas, it is often advantageous to have a half bathroom with a large tub-sink close to an outside entrance. Most people living in the country are involved in some form of outside activity, and locating a half bathroom in this position makes wash-ups and cleaning vegetables very convenient. The urban dwelling may have similar special requirements which should be outlined before plumbing work begins. Wherever possible plumbing should not be run on exterior walls, because it is difficult to insulate.

In any of these plumbing installations adequate venting is of prime importance. Rigid electrical standards are called for in such areas as the bathroom, kitchen, and laundry, and they must be taken into account. If a bedroom is to be converted into a bathroom, note the physical make-up of the room. Is there headroom for a shower, a problem in a one-and-a-half storey house. Will the ceiling beams below be affected by bathtub piping? Are the woods in the room to be painted or treated for moisture penetration? Untreated softwoods, with the exception of cedar, are extremely susceptible to dry rot. New materials, such as ceramic tile, vinyls, and quick-drying synthetic carpets, should be considered in these areas. The use of ceramic tile can be documented from before the time of Christ, and it can provide a harmonious, practical, and economical solution to the problem of what to do with counter tops and floors.

At today's plumbing rates, it is false economy to buy anything other than the highest quality fixtures. Cheap fixtures are susceptible to breakdown, and repair parts are hard to come by.

Rural dwellers have two extra areas of concern, because water supply and waste removal systems must be self-contained on the property. The original well was frequently quite shallow, only ten to twenty feet in some cases, and its use was supplemented by the collection of rainwater. By 1870, the Gilz-Well Auger Company of St. Louis, Missouri, was advertising equipment that could drill "50 ft. in one day."[7] Although this is a somewhat questionable claim, the fact remains that drilled wells were common by about this time.

Old wells must be checked for rotten covers, bacteria in the water, and hourly flows of refill. Early dug wells often cannot supply the demands of the modern house, and a new well must be sunk. New wells cost approximately ten dollars a foot, so you should allow ample leeway in your budget.

Septic tanks or aquarobic systems are used for waste disposal. Your local health inspector will advise you where and how both well and disposal system should be placed. Fifty feet apart in the case of drilled well and a hundred feet in the case of a dug well are generally accepted guidelines. Discuss the situation with the health inspector as you have with other tradesmen. Wherever possible try not to disturb mature vegetation that may form an important part of period atmosphere.

Victorian and Edwardian bathrooms were often splendid in overall decor, and many designers of these earlier times excelled in furnishing them. If the bathroom is to be restored, early fixtures and piping must be revamped. Old pipes must be checked for breakage, scaling, splits, and so on; they should be replaced with copper or plastic where necessary. Return traps and vent stacks must be free from blockage. Worn-out old gaskets and washers should be replaced, and the entire system should be flushed through and pressure checked. Old pipes may have been reduced to a fraction of their original interior diameters by years of soap scum and natural scaling. Period bathtubs can be restored with epoxies, although the availability of good replacements of the same age from the local junkyard may make repair unnecessary. Marble sink and counter tops, always a delightful and practical part

of Victorian or Edwardian period decor, can be cleaned with paint cleaners and steel wool. Heavy stains, though, may require fine sandpaper and even muriatic acid.

Prince Albert, Queen Victoria's husband, died of typhoid. Edward VII was almost killed by the same disease, reliably thought to have been caused by bad drains at the Countess of Londesborough's house. Typhoid is fairly unlikely today, but do take warning, and when restoring the bathroom of this period ensure that the waste system vents are functioning properly.

CHAPTER EIGHT

Finishing

WHAT ORIGINALLY SOWED THE SEEDS OF love for the period structure? Was it lack of funds, a previously written book on old houses, the romantic notion of life in past generations, or the collecting of antiques? Throughout previous chapters the seeds of joy have been buffeted, in some cases abused, and occasionally nurtured by the basic technical demands of the structure. The finished interior, the area where our triumphs and mistakes will be seen on a daily basis, is where for most of us these early seeds will blossom into statements of the house's personality and our own. This is no less true of the finished exterior with its complementary landscaping, but this is a more public statement of pleasure and pride in the period home.

Interior elements can be broken up into the walls and interior partitions, the ceilings, the floors, and the interior joinery. Under the heading of joinery is included mouldings, doorways, chimney pieces, wainscoting, and so on.

As outlined in Chapter 2, distinct differences in treatment will occur in the decor of the historical rehabilitation as opposed to space usage. Perhaps the single most important theme of this book has been the tracing of the historical appearance of an area before beginning work. The interior is no different.

The mood and atmosphere of early settlements in North America can be well illustrated by the etymology of the word "wainscot." Wallace Nutting, in his *Furniture of the Pilgrim Century*, informs us that, "The wain, the common English word for a large wagon . . . and the schot meaning partition were found to be the best and strongest when made of oak, and in the process of time the best oak for panelling was therefore named wainscot."[1] This dark oak, in combination with the small windows discussed in Chapter 6, must have resulted in a most dark and dreary atmosphere. By 1700, not only had larger windows been added to most houses, but whitewash was frequently applied to dark beams and plank ceilings.

PAINTS, STENCILING, AND WALLPAPERS

Colored paints came into use during the last half of the eighteenth century. Whereas early paints were primarily used for their preservative qualities, the basic pigments becoming available at this time allowed a certain freedom in the choice of decor. Early colored paints were mixed by hand and made up of four basic ingredients: linseed oil (the vehicle), white or red lead, color pigment, and Japan dryer.

Whitewash continued to be used on walls; it was a mixture of slaked lime, water, and perhaps salt or glue. "Lime whitewash is made from lime well slaked. Dissolve two and a half pounds of alum in boiling water and add it to every pailful ($2^{1}/_{4}$ gallons to $2^{1}/_{2}$ gallons) of whitewash."[2]

Other paints used during the period 1750-1800 were water-based and called distempers. The pigments, calcimine and casein, were the most common and were mixed with water and glue, milk or egg whites. The presence of calcimine is frequently discovered by the preservationist using another water-based paint, latex in today's parlance, over the old. The result: the new paint falls off. Calcimine paint must be removed before new paint is applied. It might also be added that the application of latex paints on early plaster will sometimes cause a

The color and texture of this New England farmhouse accentuate the mood of the eighteenth century. The house has been painted grey-blue.

chemical reaction resulting in bubbling; don't use
them in this situation.

Until the late Victorian period, factory-made
paints were not commonly available and the hand-
mixed variety was the norm. In spite of somewhat
primitive methods of supply and manufacture, a relatively large inventory of colors was available.
Jeanne Minhinnick, a pioneer in historical paint

research, documents that the following pigments
were obtainable and commonly used by 1820:

- Spanish brown—a dull, dark red
- Indian red—with a purple cast when imported
  from the East
- Indies—or scarlet
- carmine—a brilliant red

Extreme contrasts of vibrant colors were an integral part of decor in the first half of the nineteenth century.

- vermillion – a delicate red
- rose pink
- Prussian blue – intense blue
- blue-black
- sky-blue
- yellow ocher – either plain light or spruce dark
- chrome yellow – a rich and brilliant yellow
- patent or Turner's yellow – light yellow
- Dutch pink – a straw yellow

- ivory black – called the "best black"
- Frankfort black
- lamp black
- umber – a brown ocher
- verdigris – a blue-green
- red lead
- white lead
- turkey umber[3]

*Dramatic crotch-graining in a
Maine house, first quarter
nineteenth century.*

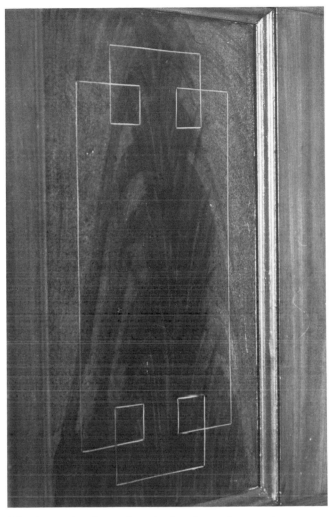

The investigation of period color schemes in any pre-1900 house can be a very interesting procedure. By definition, windows admit light, but they also reflect. In this case, they will reveal how and when individual colors were used. They should be cut in all areas of trim, near the wall and ceiling, but in relatively obscure areas so as not to mar future restoration efforts. Two methods can be used. In the first, a commercially available paint remover is placed in a saucepan. Zero-zero-zero steel wool is dipped into the remover and then applied to the surface in a circular motion. As the remover permeates the paint, a layering effect will result. This will show you the number of layers and the colors used; further dating may be possible by comparing these layers with other details of the house's history. It must be remembered, however, that these oil-based paints darken with time, and their real shade may in fact be one or two tones lighter than that discovered. Your findings should be correlated with surrounding trim and plasterwork to ascertain the color scheme used during each period.

The same result can be obtained using a second method. An Exacto knife and a magnifying glass are the tools used by professional restorationists to scrape away layers of paint, but for the layman the first method is probably the better one. Remember, paint in out-of-the-way cracks and under window sills is less susceptible to dirt and color changes. Bear in mind that many decorative nineteenth-century color treatments involved more than one coat of paint, as in stenciling, marbleizing, and woodgraining.

It is almost impossible to duplicate the mood and textural quality of early paints by contemporary means. Scarceness of materials, costs, and the dangers involved in lead-based paints,[4] have made the use of latex and alkyd paints a present-day reality. Flat, oil-based paints for walls and semi-gloss for trim are preferred, because they are technically in keeping with those of earlier periods. Latex paints are also very good, and personal preferences and job situation may dictate the type.[5]

Early colors and their relationship to one another often leave the professional, as well as the novice, in

Bird's eye graining in the John Rolph house, North Augusta, Ontario, circa 1875. This work was reputedly done by a local painter, Colonel Checkley.

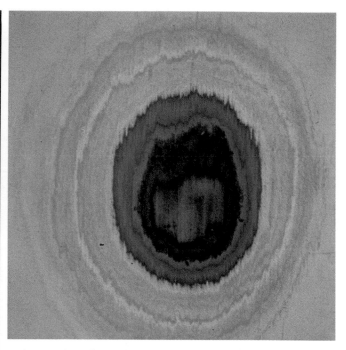

Fine steel wool and paint remover applied in a circular motion will expose earlier layers of paint. Once revealed, you will be able to gauge their approximate date.

a visual quandary. The placing of extreme tones in contrasting, unfamiliar color schemes can lead to disastrous mistakes if they are not properly coded. After ascertaining period colors by the procedures listed above, match them to a *Munsell Color Chart*, which you may be able to find in a local library. If this is unavailable, use the paint chart of a reputable paint manufacturer.

Purchase three or four sheets of birch-veneer plywood and cut them into four two-by-four pieces. Prime them with white shellac[6] and then steel wool the finish. Birch-veneer plywood is used, because it has a good, close grain. The new paints for each room should be applied in corresponding proportions. Subtle differences in sheen and texture are sometimes all that is needed to give a room the wrong feeling. Using plywood in this way will give a more accurate rendering of the finished contrast than one-inch by half-inch color chips.

When ordering contemporary paints, order by manufacturer and code number. Names differ with manufacturers, as do colors. Primers should be tinted in the same tonal value as the finished coat; failure to do so will result in an inaccurately toned finished coat. Contemporary dyes are expensive, so expect to pay a lot more for quality ultra-deep-based paints. Take note of the fact that in

*This cape house in the Saint John
River Valley exudes strength and
gaiety through its simple style and
delightful color scheme.*

The square in the center of this illustration shows the original stencil pattern; the outer portion has been repainted to imitate it. Upper Canada Village, Morrisburg, Ontario, circa 1830.

Victorian stenciling, third quarter nineteenth century.

democracies the majority rules. Pastels triumph over early colors. Contemporary driers are made for these pastels, not for paints containing large amounts of dye or color. Ultra-deep paints take a long time to dry.

"Oh what a tangled web we weave, when first we practise to deceive." Shakespeare's observation was obviously lost on the earliest North American settlers and their friends back home. It wasn't until the 1700s that fancy painting began in the Americas. Following the practices of European painters, the use of paint treatments to refine otherwise plebian woods, such as pine, became a sophisticated and popular craft. Marbleizing and scagliola[7] were highly regarded for their deceptive qualities. Graining remained popular from 1770 until the early twentieth century; meritorious examples have been

found from as late as 1945. Perhaps the most exciting aspect of fancy paint, and certainly the one of greatest popular interest, is the stenciler's art.

Wallpapers, while relatively common in upper crust circles and urban centers, were not ordinarily used in early rural homes. The cost of imported European papers soon encouraged the growth of an American industry. Plunket Fleeson, a Philadelphia merchant, reputedly was the first manufacturer in 1739. Wallpapers were readily available from the mid-1700s on, but in Canada they were not usually seen until the 1850s. The Barber Mill of Georgetown, Ontario, advertised as the largest wallpaper factory in North America by 1862.[8] Motifs were often English or French copies, such as the popular floral and oriental scenes that appeared after trade began with China during the 1800s.

Some evidence has been found of fancy painting in the Maritimes, and it is a safe assumption that the stenciler's art was also practised to some degree there. The stenciler used the basic pattern layouts of wallpapers as models. Friezes were painted in various patterns just below the ceiling. Such motifs as bells, laurel leaves, and groups of hearts and flowers added a new touch of gaiety to the parlors of homes. Moses Eaton, one of the few documented stencilers, was extremely fond of the pineapple as a symbol of hospitality.

Similarities in stencil designs can be found from Connecticut to Ontario, no doubt because of copying and the itinerant nature of many of these painters. Styles or designs were not only taken from wallpapers. Motifs were borrowed from Classical

furniture, nature, or whimsy. The stencil was cut from a piece of heavy card, which was held on a wall or floor and stippled with a stiff brush. One design might employ two or three colors, hence two or three separate paint applications. Although register marks used to line up motifs accurately have been found on some stencil patterns, most artists went by a practised eye, giving a slightly irregular charm to the overall pattern.

Floor stenciling did not begin until the early 1800s, because the habit of scrubbing the floor daily with water, sand, and sometimes a harsh soap was still very much in evidence until that time. Floors would be painted a solid color, then embellished with a simple border or a fancier design. Geometric patterns (imitation tile) evolved into the floor cloth. This was a canvas sheet, painted numerous times and decorated; it resembled today's linoleum. Spatter painting was also common as a floor finish. It involved a base coat (yellow), three or four other colors, a rag on a stick, and the literal dabbing of this stick into the paint and onto the floor.

Stenciling was not limited to early periods. It was common throughout the Victorian era and is still practised in churches today. The stenciler's colors were vibrant and intense, and the restorationist must pay attention to their tone and physical make-up. Test patterns can follow those discussed in establishing a sample scheme using plywood sheets. Stenciling can be a most inexpensive and pleasant way to decorate, since most people have the talent to do it themselves. Floors treated in this way should have a good coat of high-quality marine varnish over them to prevent excessive wear. Polyurethane finishes form a hard, plastic surface and

When this ceiling was replastered, the original decorative plasterwork was left intact.

are not recommended. Pine floors are soft, high heels will puncture the coating, and the surface will wear out in areas of regular traffic. Patching is virtually impossible.

PLASTER

Early interior walls or partitions were made with plain sheathing or planks butted together and placed either horizontally or vertically. Feather-edged sheathing was common in New England in the 1700s, while tongue-in-groove, raised-bead-joint partitions from as late as 1870 have been found in Ontario. Partitions as we know them (framing, lath, and plaster) did not appear until the mid to late 1700s. Plaster and lath were readily available at an earlier date, but because nails were made by

hand and hundreds were needed for lathing, the form was limited.

Lath can be divided into two classes: hand-split or accordion lath and the machine-made type. The first kind was made from a single board, using a mallet and froe, so the single, continuous piece of lath would "accordion" when pulled apart. Plaster, on the other hand, was applied in three coats: a scratch coat, a straightening coat, and a finish coat. When the scratch coat was troweled onto the lath, the plaster oozed between the gaps in the lath. The "keys" of plaster formed on the other side of the lath actually held the plaster on the walls. The retention of early plasterwork does much to maintain the character and feel of an early period. Decorative plaster, such as a central ceiling medallion, is extremely expensive to repair or replace, and much care must be taken to preserve it. These high costs have led to innovative reproductions.

Wood mouldings in a vast assortment of styles are available at reasonable cost from various companies. Formal chair-rails, cornices, and pediments are just a sampling of what may be obtained. Other, similar mouldings can be bought that are made in lightweight fiberglass, plastic, and foam, enabling the novice to match and repair decorative plasterwork at relatively low cost.

Plaster should be carefully examined for bulging or cracking that may be the result of structural movement or extreme temperature changes. Broken keying, sometimes caused by lath applied too close together in initial construction, may show the same symptoms, as will actual material breakdown caused by an inferior original plaster mixture. As always, moisture is usually the biggest culprit. Dampness may cause dry rot in the lath or the fastenings to rust out, which in turn will loosen the lath. Mould may form from a combination of moisture and wallpaper glue. Flaking or peeling will appear both because of extremes of moisture or extremes of dryness.

If the plasterwork in your house is missing considerable portions, explore neighborhood structures built about the same time to determine period styles. Basic procedures must be followed if repairs are in order. Cracks should be cut out and filled with a suitable material, such as Polyfilla or drywaller's Durabond. Large cracks should be built up in stages; drywall tape may help. Before filling a crack, make sure that surrounding plaster is secure. Large portions of plaster may be tightened by the use of countersunk grommets, and the grommet may then be plastered over. If large areas must be taken down, drywall of the same thickness can be used over the lath as an economical replacement. A plaster effect may be achieved on the drywall by means of texturing plasters like Dromex or Durabond. Never use the original lath if you are replastering, because the gaps or "panes" are already full and keying may not occur due to chemical resistance. Remember, the reason for buying an old house is often the charms of its irregularities. Uneven but structurally sound plasterwork is part of that charm.

EXTERIOR PAINT

During the eighteenth century, a form of thinned tar was used as an exterior preservative. As colored paint came into vogue, lead-based paints replaced this crude but effective covering. Most period houses that one encounters will have an oil-based paint on the outside, and you should repaint with a similar one.

Before beginning work, the exterior should be examined for the problems discussed in Chapter 6, then determine whether previous paints are oil or latex. Sand, scrape and, in extreme cases, burn off the old paint. Burning the old paint should only be done when detailing has been lost due to numerous coats of paint or when heavy blistering or checking has occurred. The area to be painted should be washed with a non-alkaline detergent. Coat any new wood with a suitable preservative; treat knots, end-grains, and edges with aluminum primer. All caulking and puttying of holes should be done now. Two finish coats will be necessary. Paint only above 45° F (7° C) and never in hot sun. Oil-based paints must

be applied to a dry surface. Small-pane windows take twice as long as double-pane windows. Be sure to set reasonable time limits for repainting.

STRIPPING AND SANDING

During the mid-twentieth century, the popularity of Scandinavian furniture and decor did much to create a new awareness of shape, space usage, and form in the North American mind. Although nowadays frowned upon by museums and serious collectors of Canadian furniture and architecture, the stripping of furniture, woodwork, and floors was once carried out by museum and collector alike in an attempt to fit home-grown objects into this most pleasant style. Practitioners of space rehabilitation may well still find vestiges of this fashion to their liking. Basic stripping of floors and painting walls and trim white is an immediate, clean, and economical solution to what otherwise might be a drab interior.

There are two kinds of stripping: commercial chemical removers (such as Dip and Strip) and mechanical stripping (burning, scraping, sanding). The disturbance of finishes surviving from bygone eras should be done judiciously and with extreme care. Shellac or varnish was often used as a cover over decorative paintwork. Methyl hydrate and a terry cloth rag will frequently expose a beautifully grained panel with a minimum of cost and effort. Heat guns can be used to remove paint from trim and doors, but you must be careful not to remove too much. Heat guns also darken original paints. Dry scraping with dull knives or spoons is feasible on small areas, but remember to go with the grain of the wood.

For different reasons, chemical stripping can also be employed on small areas. Once applied you have virtually no control over it, and where exceptional decorative paint is suspected, do not use this method. Once paint identification has been completed (see page 187), it is more important to overpaint with the period color than to strip everything and start fresh. The scope and complexity of precise stripping to an earlier period will tax the most fanatical preservationist. To leave earlier paints undisturbed gives future devotees grounds for accurate recording and fulfills the definition of the word "preservation." Of course, where period details have been lost, stripping may take place using one or a combination of the above methods. Experiment slowly and carefully.

The complete stripping of a structure's joinery should be done only after much thought, not only about the process but about health concerns. The most expedient method is a heat gun. After the bulk of the paint is removed, a chemical stripper can be applied. Take warning, though, that heat mixed with paint is extremely flammable. Adequate fire precautions must be taken. Chemical removers are notorious for their toxic fumes, and continuous unventilated use has been known to lead to brain damage and heart attacks. Act accordingly.

A heat gun and a scraper will layer the paint off in controlled strips. Once most of the paint has been removed and the area has cooled, a chemical remover can be liberally applied. Depending on the intricacy of the joinery, the area can be covered with newspaper, keeping the fumes in, and then wiped clean using medium to fine steel wool and assorted knives, scalpels, and scrapers. Methyl hydrate is a good, low-cost neutralizer for most commercial paint removers.

A note to would-be strippers: be prepared for what you find. As the nineteenth century progressed, that beautiful honey pine so longed for became a hodgepodge of basswood, white pine and other woods, resulting in a wide variety of color combinations. The arts of the wood grainer, although they were initially developed to lend inferior woods such as red pine a more prestigious air, continued into the Victorian and Edwardian periods for good reason.

The stripping of decorative mouldings by removing them and transferring them to hot stripping tanks usually renders the mouldings unfit for further use. Although the paint comes off, the wood is permeated with the stripping chemical. It is not visible immediately, but as regluing and repainting take place and central heating returns, chemical reactions will occur nullifying both paint and glue. Stripping in this way also tends to raise the grain, leaving a burr or fuzzy quality to the wood. The time spent sanding this down to an acceptable finish is greater than hand stripping.

Pine or hardwood floors are best finished with a drum sander and edger. Extreme care must be exercised in both cases, again for health reasons and the appearance of the completed work. Lead-based paint is poisonous, and high-speed sanders create lead dust. Speaking from personal experience, after twice fainting when using this process, I have become even more a devotee of the overpainted floor. If you are sanding, slowly travel up and down in the direction the flooring runs. Occasionally, when floors are highly irregular, going against the grain can cut through the highest ridges. Start with coarse belts and work to fine. Always be sure to adequately vent the area.

Especially in pine floors, large cracks might be present. After the floor is sanded, sweep the sawdust against the cracks so they fill up. Lightly vacuum the remainder of the sawdust, and then pour clear varnish over the cracks. Once this has dried, apply the first coat to the entire floor. When this coat has dried, buff the floor with steel wool pads on a floor polisher. Vacuum again and continue finishing. Remember, though, that joints will flex with the movement of the house. The irregularity of most period pine floors, with their traffic wear patterns and protruding knots, are part of the charm of the old house. Sanding will remove these elements.

A soaring classic of the joiner's
work, the balustrade of the Lord
house, Maine, first quarter
nineteenth century.

JOINERY

Even though the master builder was a combination of architect, craftsman, and decorator, there seemed to be a distinct difference between a carpenter, an occupation falling under the master builder heading, and the joiner, a craftsman who was a carpenter but one who specialized in finished woodwork. The joiner's work can be divided into five sections when it is approached by the preservationist: mouldings, baseboards and valances, doors, fine work, wainscoting and paneling, stairs and mantels. Mouldings and decorative trim were not common elements in the shanty or first home, but as early structures in Virginia and Quebec will attest, their skilful application was not long in coming. The craftsmen of the early 1700s did not distinguish to any great degree between interior and exterior trim, the primary influences being early Roman public buildings. Their skill is evident in the ability to adapt the overwhelming proportions of these public buildings to the lesser proportions of the private residence. The fireplace surround with its monumental appearance and broken pediment dominated the room.

What we now know as the baseboard was usually referred to as the mop board. It was added, as were so many things, more for preservation than decoration. Daily floor scrubbings with water, sand, and harsh soap, especially in the kitchen, caused rot where the sheathed walls met the floorboards. Although the skill of the joiner was well known throughout the eighteenth century, there were relatively few of these craftsmen and their products were still at a premium.

By the late 1700s, architects were favoring the more gentle lines of Greek civilization. A Neoclassi-

cal style with ovals and semi-elliptical arches seemed more suited to structures of the period. The Adam brothers, fervent believers in the Greek style, observed:

The mouldings in the remaining structures of ancient Rome are considerably less curvilineal than those of the ancient monuments of Greece. We have always given preference to the latter, and have even thought it advisable to bend them still more in many cases, particularly in interior finishings, where objects are near, and ought to be softened to the eye.[9]

As usual, practical innovations also occurred. Moulding machines appeared in urban areas as the eighteenth century drew to a close. By 1830, a machine had been developed by William Woodworth of New York that dominated planing machine design until the mid-nineteenth century. A machine that successfully and commercially produced

By the first quarter of the nineteenth century, mouldings had become very complex in profile and difficult to join at the corners of door frames with a 45-degree angle cut. Corner blocks were used to alleviate this problem.

The use of a profile gauge.

mouldings was built in 1848 by C. B. Roger & Co. of Norwich, Connecticut, in association with J. A. Fay & Co. of Keene, New Hampshire. These machines created mass-produced mouldings in a fairly wide range of styles, but in rural areas the use of hand tools survived to a much later date.

Over the years mouldings or staircase railings may have fallen out or been removed for one reason or another. These often end up in the attic or out-buildings. The travel of the missing sections can add considerable charm to the history of the house. A 1700 timber-frame house, located near North Berwick, Maine, was missing part of the staircase railing when the new owners purchased it in the 1960s. The previous owner said she had the pieces somewhere. They had been broken off one July 4th weekend when the local factory had its picnic on the grounds of the house. Some of the lads had

gotten drunk and broken the railing. She remembered searching for four days for the pieces. One was found in the garden, a few more around the house, but the last was lost. A week later, when looking out over the lake, she found the missing piece floating near the shore. She had carefully put them all together in a box, waiting for the day when they would be restored.

Reproduction or repair of period mouldings is a two-phase operation: research and manufacturing. It is imperative that adequate dimensions be obtained. Materials should be checked *in situ* for tool marks, types of fastenings, and period finishes. Heavy paint layering must be removed to obtain an accurate profile, which can be done using a profile gauge. Commercially available gauges can be hard to find and even then may be of poor quality.[10] It is advisable to make your own gauge out of soft metal.

A surplus of windows and doors in Victorian kitchens can result in limited counter space. This L-shaped counter unit solves the problem.

Although it is not always possible, removing part of the moulding to be reproduced gives the best profile of all, and for the amateur who does not have sophisticated equipment it is by far the best method. Obviously, this must be done carefully, but most mouldings were attached using soft nails, so it can be a relatively simple operation. Usually, period moulding reproduction requires custom milling, as thickness and moisture content are considerably different from today's standards. Moisture content should be between five and ten per cent. The equipment used to make these mouldings may only be a small part of a larger woodworking shop or mill. Discussions should be held to insure quality and correct methodology. The costs for custom mouldings will vary from area to area and detail to detail. Get a firm quote before work is begun. It is wise in your overall plan to identify moulding requirements and finish details at an early stage. It is tempting, as the project nears completion and finances are strained, to accept second-rate methods. Remember that these elements will be seen daily. Utmost care should be taken in repair or reproduction.

HARDWARE

Nothing is more disturbing to the eye than incorrect fastenings and hardware. Compromises will obviously be necessary in the face of the contemporary demands of our society, but a singular lack of imagination is often visible in this area. Before 1800 the blacksmith was the hardware man. He made everything from nails to locks. His talents, like those of other craftsmen, peaked in North America during the eighteenth century, although, as usual, excellent

examples have survived made as late as the 1860s. By 1800, the butt hinge had been invented (its actual date is 1775) and mass-production allowed design adaptations in such things as the hanging of doors. That is, earlier drop, rat-tail, and strap hinges all required the door to be hung on the outside of an object in a basic slot and pin arrangement. The butt hinge made possible such things as the inset door and the like.

Wherever possible, period hardware should be used, although excellent reproductions are available from many sources. Originals may be obtained from auctions, antique dealers, or restoration specialists. A problem with period hardware arises where security is necessary, but reproduction locks made to today's standards have been designed. Cylinder locks, inset and painted to match a door, can be nearly invisible and relatively inoffensive. Win-

A Suffolk latch, eighteenth century.

A Suffolk latch in the style of the French Regime of Quebec, mid-1700s.

Pull and escutcheon, first quarter nineteenth century.

A Norfolk latch, last quarter eighteenth century.

Iron door knocker, first quarter nineteenth century.

Wishbone latch set, first quarter nineteenth century.

An appropriately appointed bed-room.

The formality of the richly grained doors is echoed in the furnishings of this Neoclassical dining room.

The parlor of the early house was often sparsely furnished.

Detail of a three-batten plank door using clinched rose-headed nails as the fastenings and cast butt hinges.

dows may be fastened securely with a traditional window pin, a small pin inserted through the sash into the frame. Shutters also provide good security. The Indian shutter of New England once fended off arrows; they can also foil the contemporary burglar.

ADDITIONS

Rising energy costs are forcing us to live more in the manner of our forefathers, a movement which I for one wholly support. Smaller houses can be perfectly adequate, particularly in view of the fact that most families live in the kitchen, bathroom, and bedroom. Even so, it is sometimes necessary to construct an addition to the period structure. The same axioms apply whether you are engaged in historical rehabilitation or space usage. Attention must be paid to exterior harmony, proportion, and texture

*This linking addition complements
both the house and the carriage
shed in scale, form, and texture.*

of materials as they relate to the original building. You must ask yourself the same basic questions as in Chapter 2. The addition will be completely new, of course, but the routing of heating, plumbing, and wiring from the original part of the house must be adequately mapped out. Can the mechanical services support additional loads? The effect of the addition on traditional traffic patterns must also be investigated. Will the landscaping be drastically disturbed? Factors of use versus cost must be carefully worked out. Don't forget to record what you have done for the next tenant in the history of the house.

*A modern addition to a period
house must be sympathetic to
already established design and
landscape.*

This 1930s verandah has been turned into a year-round living space.

The large amount of open space in this Edwardian town house is accented by the eclectic decor chosen by its owners.

The subtle elegance of the Neoclassical parlor provides a suitable backdrop for good furnishings from any period.

Living with the past, rather than re-creating it, is the essence of good historical rehabilitation.

*Although exposed brickwork may
be of some aesthetic appeal, the
original plaster provided excellent
thermal and sound insulation.*

Fencing and wooden pathways were nearly always a part of the landscape of nineteenth-century domestic architecture.

LANDSCAPING

In the enthusiasm to begin work on the house, one of its most significant aspects is frequently ignored. A contemporary realtor's term, "curb appeal," concisely, if somewhat commonly, sums up the importance of landscaping. Eighty per cent of all real estate sales are reputedly made on the basis of that first external impression.

The same qualities and charms that one finds in the structure are often mirrored in a mature landscape from a bygone era. It is surprisingly easy to document designs and traffic flow patterns on the basis of this landscape. The position of the well, the outhouse, the woodpile, or the planting of trees in a systematic arrangement all may add to your knowledge of earlier lifestyles.

Initially, landscaping in North America was based on European models. However, gardens laid out in geometric patterns surrounded by small, tight fences must have seemed uncommonly formal in a more primitive setting. As settlement progressed, the natural vegetation of North America influenced the look of the garden. In 1806, Bernard McMahon published *The American Gardener's Catalogue*. He advocated rural open spaces spotted with trees and clumps of shrubs highlighted by meandering walkways. Andrew Jackson Downing, a man of incredible influence in several areas, published an 1841 treatise on the theory and practice of landscape gardening. As in architecture, his ideas shaped the North American landscape. Lawns were planted around the house, complemented by circular flower beds designed for the delight of inhabitants and visitors alike. The use of urns and water as decorative parts of the landscape formed further aspects of Downing's work.

The Victorian landscape often grew around a single theme. The general weightiness of the era was echoed in the somewhat cluttered but quite beautiful Victorian garden. Just as the China trade influenced interior decor, so too it affected the North American garden. Previously unheard of flowers and herbs grew in profusion.

The landscapes must be analyzed at the time of the initial site inspection. A site plan should be drawn up showing property boundaries, structures, types and locations of fences, access (driveways, walks), utilities (water drains), and underground lines. Placements of flower beds, trees, and vegetable gardens should also be recorded, along with the identities of particular plants where possible. Don't forget to include noteworthy views created by these placements.

In planning the house, it is important to marry past history with contemporary requirements. Snow clearance, sidewalk build-up, and modern traffic patterns all make demands on mature landscaping. In the garden as in the house, you should be aiming for the character of the period. Those who planned and planted the early landscape would no doubt envy the mature gardens that have evolved.

It is precisely this marriage, this harmony of past and present, that makes the preservation of period buildings so intensely satisfying. Living within this harmony, after having worked and thought and considered, can be one of life's purest joys. All that is needed is a suitable case for treatment.

Appendix: Resources

HARDWARE

Les Agences en Quincaillerie
Aird
Hardware Agencies
517 Lebeau
St. Laurent, Quebec H4N 1S2

Antique Hardware
24 Birch Avenue
Toronto, Ontario M4V 1C8
A complete line of decorative and finishing hardware.

Baldwin Hardware Manufacturing Corp.
841 Wyomissing Boulevard
Reading, Pennsylvania 19603
Reproduction eighteenth-century hardware.

Horton Brasses
P. O. Box 95
Nooks Hill Road
Cromwell, Connecticut 06416
A large selection of finishing hardware from all periods.

The Renovators Supply
71 Northfield Road
Millers Falls, Maine 01349
Hardware and some tools.

Ritter & Son
P. O. Box 907
119 E. Alice Avenue
Campbell, California 95008
Fine reproduction cast or wrought iron.

MAGAZINES AND REFERENCE BOOKS

City Magazine
Charlottetown Group Publishing Inc.
35 Britain Street
Toronto, Ontario M5A 1R7

Historic Preservation
National Trust for Historic Preservation
748 Jackson Place N.W.
Washington, D. C. 20006

Iron Horse Antiques, Inc.
Reference Book Division
R.R. #2
Poultney, Vermont 05764

The Old House Journal
69A Seventh Avenue
Brooklyn, New York 11217

MASONRY

Historic Boulevard Services
1520 West Jackson Boulevard
Chicago, Illinois 60607
Suppliers of terra cotta chimney pots.

ORGANIZATIONS

Association for the Preservation of Technology
Box 2487
Station D
Ottawa, Ontario K1P 5W6

Heritage Canada
P. O. Box 1358
Station B
Ottawa, Ontario K1P 5R4

National Trust for Historic Preservation
H.Q. 740
748 Jackson Place N.W.
Washington, D.C.

PAINT

Old Fashioned Milk Paint Company
P. O. Box 222
Groton, Massachusetts 01450
Manufacturers of paints in period colors.

Turco Coatings
Wheatland and Mellon Streets
Phoenixville, Pennsylvania 19460
Manufacturers of paints in period colors.

PLASTER ORNAMENTS
Decorator's Supply Company
3610 S. Morgan Street
Chicago, Illinois 60609

Focal Point Inc.
3760 Lower Roswell Road
Marietta, Georgia 30060

PLUMBING
Waltec Industries Ltd.
Wallaceburg, Ontario N8A 4L9
Suppliers of aquarobic waste disposal systems.

SCHOOLS AND WORKSHOPS
Algonquin College
1385 Woodroffe Avenue
Nepean, Ontario K2E 5L2

Eastfield Village
P. O. Box 145
East Nassau, New York 12062

International Center for the Study of the
Preservation of Cultural Property (ICCROM)
13 Via di San Michele
Rome, Italy

Restore Skills Training Program
30 Rockefeller Plaza
New York, New York 10020

St. Lawrence College
Restoration and Preservation Technology Program
20 Parkdale Avenue
Brockville, Ontario K6V 5X3

TOOLS
Lee Valley Tools
P. O. Box 6295
Ottawa, Ontario K2A 1T4
Suppliers of fine and hard-to-find tools, both new and antique. Antique hardware is occasionally available.

Woodcraft Supply Corporation
313 Montvale Avenue
Woburn, Massachusetts 01801

WALLPAPERS
Watts and Co., Ltd.
7 Tufton Street
Westminster
London, England SW1P 3QB
Specialists in Victorian wallpapers.

WOOD
Architectural Lumber Specialties
Dana, Deck and Laminates Inc.
Lopez, Washington 98261
Suppliers of fancy shingles and shakes.

Canadian Wood Council
170 Laurier Avenue West
Ottawa, Ontario K1P 5V5
Publishers of the "Metric Manual for Wood Products."

Council of Forest Industries of
British Columbia
1500/1055 West Hastings Street
Vancouver, British Columbia V6E 2H1
Publishers of the "Plywood Handbook."

Kensington Historical Company
P. O. Box 87
East Kensington, New Hampshire 03827
Suppliers of period building materials.

Parker Imports
95 Montpellier Boulevard
St. Laurent, Quebec H4M 2G4
Importers of a wood moisture meter.

Notes

THE PHILOSOPHY OF PRESERVATION (pages 10 to 23)

1 A. J. Downing, *The Architecture of Country Houses* (New York: Dover Publications, 1969), pp. 2-3.

THE BUILDERS (pages 24 to 37)

1 Jean S. McGill, *A Pioneer History of the County of Lanark* (Toronto: self-published, 1968), p. 17.

2 Jean Palardy, *The Furniture of French Canada* (Toronto: Macmillan Co. of Canada, 1963), p. 380.

3 Andrea Palladio (1518-1580) was an Italian architect who imitated ancient Roman architecture without strict adherence to Classical principles. His handbook of designs was extremely influential in the eighteenth century, particularly in England, where a translation appeared in 1714.

LIFESTYLES (pages 38 to 51)

1 Frances Phipps, *Colonial Kitchens, Their Furnishings and Their Gardens* (New York: Hawthorn Books, 1972), p. 27.

2 *Ibid*.

3 For a thorough history of bedding, see Ruth McKendry, *Quilts and Other Bed Coverings in the Canadian Tradition* (Toronto: Van Nostrand Reinhold, 1979).

4 Jeanne Minhinnick, *At Home in Upper Canada* (Toronto: Clarke, Irwin & Company, 1970), p. 18.

5 A good idea of early furnishings may be gotten from Howard Pain's *The Heritage of Upper Canadian Furniture* (Toronto: Van Nostrand Reinhold, 1978) and Wallace Nutting's *Furniture Treasury*, 2 vols. (New York: The Macmillan Co., 1928).

THE STRUCTURE (pages 72 to 113)

1 Jean S. McGill, *A Pioneer History of the County of Lanark* (Toronto: self published, 1968), p. 28.

2 According to Parks Canada.

3 Jean Palardy, *The Furniture of French Canada* (Toronto: Macmillan Co. of Canada, 1963), p. 22.

4 Jean S. McGill, *A Pioneer History of the County of Lanark*, p. 230.

5 Henry Russell, quoted in Andy Davey, et al., *Architecture: Nineteenth and Twentieth Centuries* (Edinburgh: Paul Harris Publishing, 1978), p. 3.

6 Edwin C. Guillet, *Pioneer Arts and Crafts* (Toronto: University of Toronto Press, 1968), p. 42.

7 Fiske Kimball, *Domestic Architecture of the American Colonies and of the Early Republic* (New York: Dover Publications, n.d.), p. 39.

8 *Ibid*., p. 37.

9 My thanks to Dr. Ralph Price for this information, which is recorded in a family history.

THE EXTERIOR (pages 114 to 145)

1 Frances Phipps, *Colonial Kitchens, Their Furnishings and Their Gardens* (New York: Hawthorn Books, 1972), p. 6.

2 Marion Nicholl Rawson, *Sing Old House* (New York: E. P. Dutton, 1934), p. 85.

3 A. J. Downing, *The Architecture of Country Houses* (New York: Dover Publications, 1969), p. 84.

MECHANICAL SYSTEMS AND THE PERIOD STRUCTURE (pages 146 to 179)

1 Susanna Moodie, *Roughing It in the Bush, or Forest Life in Canada* (1852; rpt. Toronto: Bell & Cockburn, 1913), p. 550.

2 Peter Kalm, *Travels in North America* (Warrington, England: n. pub., 1812), p. 86.

3 F.C. Wurtele, "Historical Records of the St. Maurice Forges," *Transactions of the Royal Society of Canada* (1886). Vol. 4, Sec. II, pp. 77-89.

4 Jeanne Minhinnick, *At Home in Upper Canada* (Toronto: Clarke, Irwin & Company, 1970), p. 99.

5 Count Rumford, *Essays: Political, Economical and Philosophical* (London, 1795).

6 Leonard de Uries and Ilonka Van Amstel, *The Wonderful World of American Advertisements*, 1865-1908 (London: John Murray, 1972), p. 81.

7 *Ibid.*, p. 79.

FINISHING (pages 180 to 214)

1 Wallace Nutting, *Furniture of the Pilgrim Century* (1921-1924; rpt. New York: Dover Publications, 1965), Vol. I, p. 281.

2 John F. Zirkle, "The Refinishing Clinic: A Whitewash Formula," *The Old House Journal* (September 1979), p. 107.

3 Jeanne Minhinnick, *At Home in Upper Canada* (Toronto: Clarke, Irwin & Company, 1970), p. 125.

4 To determine whether paint is lead-based, scrape a bit into a solution of five to eight per cent sodium suphide and water. If the solution turns black, the paint is lead-based.

5 There are at least two companies that specialize in period paints. Both are located in the United States. The first is Turco Coatings, Wheatland and Mellon Streets, Phoenixville, Pennsylvania 19460, and the second is the Old Fashioned Milk Paint Company, P.O. Box 222, Groton, Massachusetts 01450. Letters to them will obtain color chips and details.

6 Prepared shellac is expensive, but you can buy shellac flakes in bulk from Lee Valley Tools, P.O. Box 6295, Ottawa, Ontario K2A 1T4 at much lower prices. Mixed with methyl hydrate, the flakes are just as good as the prepared mixture.

7 Scagliola is a more complex technique than marbleizing. Colored plaster of paris is mixed with pieces of marble, flint, etc. It was used mainly on larger architectural features such as columns and pilasters or for elaborate insets in fireplaces.

8 In the *Grand Trunk Directory* of 1862.

9 Robert and James Adam, *The Works in Architecture of Robert and James Adam* (London: T. Becket, 1773-1774), Vol. 2, Book I, p. 7.

10 This is ordinarily true, but Lee Valley Tools does carry an excellent if expensive profile gauge; see note 6.

Glossary

Adze   A tool used to dress a hewn beam. Similar to an axe but with the cutting edge at a right angle to the handle.

Aquarobic   A domestic sewage disposal system utilizing an electric motor to accelerate waste breakdown. Considerably less weeping tile, hence considerably less total area, is required compared to a conventional system.

Ashlar   The outside face of a wall of cut stone. In *coursed ashlar* the stone is of uniform size, and the joints are continuous. In *broken ashlar* the stone is irregularly dressed, but the joints resemble *coursed ashlar*.

Auger   A cutting instrument or bore.

Balloon frame   A method of wood-frame construction in which the studs extend in one piece from the foundation wall to the top plate supporting the roof.

Balustrade   A low parapet.

Bargeboard (or Gingerbread)   A decorated board on a gable edge or eave line.

Board and batten   A vertical form of cladding using eight-to-twelve-inch planks, butt-joined with a two-inch batten over the seam.

Bond stone   In a masonry wall, a stone facing on both sides and running through the wall tying the sides together.

Bond timbers   Strengthening or reinforcing timbers.

Braced frame   A nineteenth-century system of balloon and timber-frame construction.

Broad axe   An axe with a short, bent handle and a cant in the head on the same side as the bend. Used for hewing or squaring logs into beams; not a finishing tool.

Buck   A rough window frame, before the sash is installed.

Came   An H-shaped lead strip used to hold window glass in seventeenth- and eighteenth-century North America.

Casement   A window with side-hinged sashes.

Chair-rail   Interior moulding applied along a wall (thirty to thirty-five inches from the floor) to prevent chair backs from marking the wall.

Check   A longitudinal crack caused by too rapid seasoning.

Cladding   The skin of a building, as in shingles or clapboard; not a structural element.

Clapboard   A horizontal, exterior wood finish, shaped or overlapped to form a weatherproof cladding.

Collar tie   A tie between two rafters used to provide intermediate support.

Colombage pierrotte   A half-timber house with rubble-stone infill.

Corbelling   A method of laying brick or stone to achieve an angle or an arch but on a horizontal plane.

Cornice   A projection crowning a building.

Cross and Bible   The description of the panel distribution in a Georgian six-panel door.

Cross-cut saw   A saw with two sets of teeth crossing each other diagonally.

Crown glass   Early glass was blown and spun into a flat disc. The best was called Crown glass. Irregularities and the pontil iron mark are telltale signs.

Dormer   A vertical window in the slope of a roof.

Double-hung   A window with vertically sliding double sections.

Dovetail   The end of a beam or log cut in a wedge shape to interlock with another; looks like a bird's tail.

Drawknife   A knife with handles at either end used for dressing rough wood.

Eave The horizontal edge of a roof.

Facade The face of a building.

Fascia A flat band nailed to the ends of rafters, usually with ornate cornice detailing.

Fenestration The placement and trim of windows and exterior doors.

Finial A pointed ornament at the apex of a gable, pediment, or roof edge.

Gable The upper, triangular-shaped portion of the end wall of a building.

Gallery A long porch across a facade.

Gambrel roof A gable roof with a double pitch or two slopes on each of two sides.

Gesso A mixture of plaster and glue.

Gimlet A boring tool with a cross-handle at one end and a worm or screw at the other.

Gingerbread *See* Bargeboard.

Half-timbering As a surface treatment, wooden members with plaster or stucco infill.

Header Bricks or other masonry units laid across a wall so their ends show.

Hip roof A roof sloped on all four sides.

Infill Random material used for fill; rubble in a cavity-stone wall.

Joist One of a series of parallel framing members supporting floor and ceiling loads.

Lancet A narrow, pointed window.

Light A pane of glass in a window. The term is a holdover from the time when windows had neither frame nor glass.

Lintel A horizontal structural member which supports the load over an opening, such as a door or window.

Mansard roof A variation of a hip roof with a steep lower slope (which may be curved) and a flatter upper section.

Marbleize The use of paint to simulate the appearance of marble. A Neoclassical fashion first popular in eighteenth-century France and England. *See* Scagliola.

Mortise and tenon The mortise is a cutout to receive the tenon, while the tenon is the end of another piece of lumber shaped to fit a mortise.

Mullion A perpendicular member which divides lights of glass in windows or doors.

Munton bar A horizontal member which divides lights of glass in windows or doors.

Noggin Brickwork built up between wooden quarters of framing.

Palladian An arch-headed window flanked by narrower, shorter, square-headed windows.

Pargeting A thin coat of plaster applied to stone or brick to form a smooth or decorative surface.

Parging Stuccoing on foundations to form a watertight seal.

Pediment A gable of moderate pitch with the cornice carried across at its base and up the raking sides. It may be triangular, segmental, broken, or scrolled.

Pilaster A vertical, rectangular member projecting slightly from a wall.

Point A metal fastener used to hold panes of glass in place. In masonry, the process of finishing the joints.

Portico A porch with pillars or columns.

Quarry A small, lozenge-shaped or rectangular piece of glass used in early windows.

Quarter The English term for stud.

Rafter   One of a series of structural members in a roof. The principal rafter is the beam forming the slope of the roof truss.

Rehabilitation   The process of utilizing a period building. Historical rehabilitation attempts to capture the mood of the period; adaptive rehabilitation makes use of existing space within the structure.

Restoration   Returning a building, in every detail, to its earliest or architecturally most interesting period.

Return   The continuation of a moulding at a right angle on an adjacent surface.

Rip-rap   Stones or similar material used on slopes to prevent erosion.

Rubble-stone   Roughly dressed field stone.

Saddle   In log buildings, a block of wood cut to straddle a base log where no intersecting joint (dovetail) can be made, as in window and door openings.

Scagliola   A technique more complicated than marbleizing which uses colored plaster of paris mixed with pieces of marble, flint, etc.

Shake   A split (not sawn) shingle for siding or roofing.

Sheathing   Lumber or a facsimile used on the exterior to cover the framework.

Sidelight   A glazed panel adjacent to a door.

Six-over-six window   A term describing the number and design of lights in a double-hung window; hence twelve-over-twelve or nine-over-nine.

Soffit   The underside of a projection, such as a cornice or architrave.

Spalling   The surface deterioration of brick or stone characterized by flaking.

Stencil   A thin sheet of card or metal in which one or more holes has been cut so that the shape of the hole, figure, or letter may be transferred to another object when the stencil is painted over.

Stud   One of a series of wooden structural members that supports walls or partitions.

Surround   The joinery around architectural openings.

Tick   The cloth case of a mattress or pillow stuffed with hair, straw, corn husks, or feathers.

Tie beam   A beam connecting the feet of the principal rafters of a truss to prevent them from spreading.

Timber frame   A system of construction where posts and beams support the load, not the walls.

Transom   A horizontal bar between the top of a window or door and the structural opening; the section above is a transom light or panel.

Truncated   Abruptly terminated; having the top or end cut off.

Truss   Historically, a triangle formed by two rafters and a tie beam.

Wainscot   Interior paneling commonly extending thirty inches from the floor; a combination of mop board and chair-rail in one.

Weeping tile   Buried tile runs used to dispose of water or waste runoff.

Whip saw   A long, narrow, two-handed saw for curved work.

Bibliography

ARCHITECTURE

ADAM, ROBERT, and JAMES ADAM. *The Works in Architecture of Robert and James Adam*. London: T. Becket, 1773-74.

BICKNELL, A. J., and WILLIAM T. COMSTOCK. *Victorian Architecture: Two Pattern Books*. Watkins Glen, New York: Atheneum Publishers, 1976.

BLUMENSON, JOHN G. *Identifying American Architecture*. Nashville, Tennessee: American Association for State and Local History, 1977.

BURDEN, ERNEST. *Living Barns*. New York: New York Graphic Society Books, 1977.

CLARKE, HAROLD. *Georgian Dublin*. Dublin: Eason and Son, 1976.

DAVEY, ANDY, ET AL. *Architecture: Nineteenth and Twentieth Centuries*. Edinburgh: Paul Harris Publishing, 1978.

——————. *The Care and Conservation of Georgian Houses*. Edinburgh: Paul Harris Publishing, 1978.

DOWNING, A.J. *The Architecture of Country Houses*. New York: Dover Publications, 1969.

FAULKNER, ANN. *Without Our Past*. Toronto: University of Toronto Press, 1977.

GILLIAT, MARY. *English Style*. London: Bodley Head, 1967.

GOWANS, ALAN. *Building Canada*. Toronto: Oxford University Press, 1966.

HUMPHREYS, BARBARA, and MEREDITH SYKES. *The Buildings of Canada*. Montreal: Reader's Digest Association, Canada, 1974.

ISHAM, NORMAN M. *A Glossary of Architectural Terms*. Watkins Glen, New York: American Life Foundation and Study Institute, 1978.

KIMBALL, FISKE. *Domestic Architecture of the American Colonies and of the Early Republic*. New York: Dover Publications, n.d.

Late Victorian Architectural Details. Watkins Glen, New York: American Life Foundation and Study Institute, 1978.

LESARRD, MICHEL, and HUGUETTE MARQUIS. *Encyclepedia de la Maison Québecoise*. Ottawa: Les Editions de l' Homme, 1972.

MACRAE, MARION. *The Ancestral Roof*. Toronto: Clarke, Irwin & Company, 1963.

MERCER, HENRY C. *The Dating of Old Houses*. Watkins Glen, New York: American Life Foundation and Study Institute, 1978.

PHILLIPS, R. A. J. *Up the Streets of Ontario*. Ottawa: Heritage Canada, 1976.

PIERSON, WILLIAM H., JR. *American Buildings and Their Architects*. Garden City, New York: Doubleday and Company, 1978.

RICHARDSON, DOUGLAS. *Architecture in Ontario*. Toronto: Ontario Ministry of Culture and Recreation, 1976.

ROTHERY, SEAN. *Everyday Buildings of Ireland*. Dublin: College of Technology, 1975.

STOKES, PETER JOHN. *Old Niagara-on-the-Lake*. Toronto: University of Toronto Press, 1971.

TALLMADGE, THOMAS E. *The Story of Architecture in America*. rev. ed. New York: W. W. Norton & Co., 1936.

CONSTRUCTION

ASHURST, JOHN, and FRANCIS G. DIMES. *Stone Building: Its Use and Potential Today*. London: Architectural Press, 1977.

BLACKBURN, GRAHAM. *Illustrated Housebuilding*. Woodstock, New York: Overlook Press, 1974.

BLACKWELL, DUNCAN S. *The Complete Book of Outdoor Masonry*. Pennsylvania: Tab Books, n.d.

CHING, FRANCIS D. K. *Building Construction Illustrated*. New York: Van Nostrand Reinhold, 1975.

CLIDERO, ROBERT K., and KENNETH H. SHARPE. *Applications of Electrical Construction*. Don Mills, Ontario: General Publishing, 1975.

Complete Do-It-Yourself Manual. Montreal: Reader's Digest Association, Canada, 1973.

MAGUIRE, BYRON W. *Carpentry for Residential Construction*. Reston, Virginia: Reston Publishing Co., 1975.

Plastering Skill and Practice. Chicago: American Technical Society, [1978].

VIVIAN, JOHN. *Building Stone Walls*. Vermont: Greenway Publishing, 1976.

WAGNER, WILLIS H. *Modern Carpentry*. South Holland, Illinois: Goodheart – Willcox Co., 1976.

_____. *Modern Woodworking*. South Holland, Illinois: Goodheart – Willcox Co., 1974.

HEATING

Keeping the Heat In. Ottawa: Energy, Mines and Resources Canada, 1976.

KURKA, NORMA S., and JAN NAAR. *Design for a Limited Planet: Living with Natural Energy*. New York: Ballantine Books, 1976.

RUMFORD, COUNT. *Essays: Political, Economical and Philosophical*. London, 1795.

SMITH, BAIRD M. "Conserving Energy in Historic Buildings." *Preservation Briefs No. 3*, U.S. Department of the Interior (April 1978), pp. 1-8.

VIVIAN, JOHN. *Wood Heat*. Emmaus, Pennsylvania: Rodale Press, 1976.

IRON

GERFIN, W. *The Blacksmith*. Harrisburg, Pennsylvania: Pennsylvania History and Museum Commission, 1976.

SLOANE, ERIC. *A Museum of Early American Tools*. New York: Ballantine Books, 1973.

STREETER, DONALD. "Early American Wrought Iron Hardware." *Association for the Preservation of Technology* (forthcoming 1980).

UNDERWOOD, GRAHAME, and JOHN PLANCK. *A Handbook of Architectural Ironmongery*. London: Architectural Press, 1977.

ZIMELLI, UMBERTO, and GIOVANNI VERGERIO. *Decorative Ironwork*. London: Hamlyn Publishing Group, 1969.

LANDSCAPE

FAVRETTI, RUDY J., and JOY PUTMAN FAVRETTI. *Landscapes and Gardens for Historic Buildings*. Nashville, Tennessee: American Association for State and Local History, 1978.

MCHARG, IAN L. *Design with Nature*. Garden City, New York: Doubleday & Co., 1969.

STEWART, JOHN J. "Historic Landscapes and Gardens." *Technical Leaflet 80*, American Association for State and Local History (November 1974), pp. 32-48.

LIGHTING

HAYWARD, ARTHUR H. *Colonial and Early American Lighting*. Toronto: Dover Publications, 1962.

MYERS, DENYS PETER. *Gas Lighting in America: A Guide for Historic Preservation*. Washington, D.C.: U.S. Department of the Interior, 1978.

Westinghouse Lighting Handbook. Dorval, Quebec: Westinghouse Canada, 1976.

PAINT

MINHINNICK, JEANNE. "Some Personal Observations on the Use of Paint in Early Ontario." *Association for the Preservation of Technology*, Vol. VII, No. 2 (1975), p. 13.

WARING, JANET. *Early American Stencil Decorations*. Watkins Glen, New York: Century House, 1937.

WELSH, FRANK S. "A Methodology for Exposing and Preserving Architectural Graining." *Association for the Preservation of Technology*, Vol. VIII, No. 2 (1976), p. 71.

ZIRKLE, JOHN F. "The Refinishing Clinic: A Whitewash Formula." *The Old House Journal* (September 1979), p. 107.

ZUCKER, HOWARD. "Graining." *The Old House Journal* (June 1975), pp. 10-22.

PRESERVATION

BULLOCK, ORIN M. *The Restoration Manual*. Norwalk, Connecticut: Silvermin Publishers, 1966.

COBB, HUBBARD H. *How to Buy and Remodel the Older House*. New York: Collier Books, 1965.

FINLEY, GERALD. *In Praise of Older Buildings*. Kingston, Ontario: Frontenac Historic Foundation, 1976.

FRACCHIA, CHARLES A., and JEREMIAH O. BRAGSTAD. *Converted into Houses*. London: Penguin Books, 1976.

GALT, GEORGE. *Investing in the Past: A Report on the Profitability of Heritage Conservation*. Ottawa: Heritage Canada, 1974.

Guidelines for Rehabilitating Old Buildings. Washington, D.C.: U.S. Department of Housing and Urban Development, 1977.

HAYNES, ROBERT E. *A Bibliography of Historic Preservation*. Washington, D.C.: National Park Service, 1977.

HEARN, JOHN. *The Canadian Old House Catalogue*. Toronto: Van Nostrand Reinhold, 1980.

INSALL, DONALD W. *The Care of Old Buildings Today*. London: The Architectural Press, 1972.

LITTLE, NINA FLETCHER. *Floor Coverings in New England Before* 1850. Norwalk, Connecticut: Old Sturbridge, 1967.

MACK, ROBERT C. "The Cleaning and Waterproof Coating of Masonry Buildings." *Preservation Brief No. 1*, U.S. Department of the Interior (April 1978), pp. 1-4.

——————. *Repointing Mortar Joints in Historic Buildings*. Washington, D.C.: National Park Service, 1976.

MCKEE, HARLEY J. *Introduction to Early American Masonry*. Washington, D.C.: Columbia University Press, 1973.

The Old House Journal Catalog. New York: The Old House Journal Corporation, 1979.

PAPIAN, WILLIAM N. "Insulation in Old Houses." *The Old House Journal*, Part 1 (August 1976), pp. 14-23; Part 2 (September 1976), pp. 31-43.

PHILLIPS, MORGAN W., and JUDITH E. SELWYN. *Epoxies for Wood Repairs in Historic Buildings*. Washington, D.C.: Office of Archeology and Historic Preservation, 1978.

PRUDON, THEODORE H. M. "Wooden Structural Members: Some Recent European Preservation Methods." *Association for the Preservation of Technology*, Vol. III, No. 1 (1975), p. 5

RAWSON, MARION NICHOLL. *Sing Old House*. New York: E. P. Dutton, 1934.

STEPHEN, GEORGE. *Remodeling Old Houses*. New York: Alfred A. Knopf, 1974.

STUMES, PAUL. "The Application of Epoxy Resins for the Restoration of Historic Structures." *Association for the Preservation of Technology*, Vol III, No. 1 (1975), p. 6.

WATSON, JOYCE N. "Tracing the History of a House." *Ontario Library Review* (March 1976), pp. 82-96.

WEAVER, MARTIN R. *The Conservation of Wood in Historic Buildings*. Ottawa: Department of Indian and Northern Affairs, 1978.

ROOMS

CONRAN, TERENCE. *The Bed and Bath Book*. New York: Crown Publishers, 1978.

——————. *The Kitchen Book*. New York: Crown Publishers, 1977.

PHIPPS, FRANCES. *Colonial Kitchens, Their Furnishings and Their Gardens*. New York: Hawthorn Books, 1972.

RIBALTA, MARTA, ed. *Habitat: El Dormitoro — The Bedroom — La Chambre à Coucher*. Barcelona: Editorial Blume, 1975.

——————. *Habitat: La Salle de Estor — The Livingroom — La Salle de Séjour*. Barcelona: Editorial Blume, 1975.

GENERAL

CRAWFORD, PATRICIA. *Homesteading: A Practical Guide to Living Off the Land*. New York: Collier Macmillan Co., 1975.

GUILLET, EDWIN C. *Pioneer Arts and Crafts*. Toronto: University of Toronto Press, 1968.

KALM, PETER. *Travels in North America*. Warrington, England: n. pub., 1812.

MCGILL, JEAN S. *A Pioneer History of the County of Lanark*. Toronto: (self-published, 1968).

MCKENDRY, RUTH. *Quilts and Other Bed Coverings in the Canadian Tradition*. Toronto: Van Nostrand Reinhold, 1979.

MINHINNICK, JEANNE. *At Home in Upper Canada*. Toronto: Clarke, Irwin & Company, 1970.

MOODIE, SUSANNA. *Roughing It in the Bush, or Forest Life in Canada*. 1852; rpt. Toronto: Bell & Cockburn, 1913.

NUTTING, WALLACE. *Furniture of the Pilgrim Century*. 1921-1924; rpt. New York: Dover Publications, 1965.

——————— . *Furniture Treasury*. 2 vols. New York. The Macmillan Co., 1928.

PAIN, HOWARD. *The Heritage of Upper Canadian Furniture*. Toronto: Van Nostrand Reinhold, 1978.

PALARDY, JEAN. *The Furniture of French Canada*. Toronto: Macmillan Co. of Canada, 1963.

SPENCE, HILDA, and KELVIN SPENCE. *A Guide to Early Canadian Glass*. Don Mills, Ontario: Longmans, 1966.

STEVENS, GERALD. *Early Ontario Glass*. Toronto: University of Toronto Press, 1965.

DE URIES, LEONARD, and ILONKA VAN AMSTEL. *The Wonderful World of American Advertisements*. London: John Murray, 1972.

WURTELE, F.C. "Historical Records of the St. Maurice Forges." *Transactions of the Royal Society of Canada*, Vol 4, Sec. II (1886), pp. 77-89.

Index

Adam Brothers, 27, 30, 122, 158, 198
Additions, 206-08
The American Gardener's Catalogue, 212
Analysis of structure, 70
The Architecture of Country Houses, 140
Armoire, Dutch, 48
Ash, 90
At Home in Upper Canada, 42
Attics, 132, 162-63, 166, 168, 199

Balustrades, 197-98
Barber Mill, 190
Bargeboards, 14
Baseboards, 80, 157, 174, 198
Basements, 74-75, 77, 79-80, 85, 111, 121, 137-38, 160,
    163, 166, 171
Bathrooms, 168, 176-79, 206
Beams, 18, 78, 80-81, 85, 90, 111, 173, 175, 182. *See also*
    Joists
    epoxics for, 85
    load-bearing, 81
    splicing, 85
Bedrooms, 40, 42, 44, 149, 151, 204, 206
Bell, Andrew, 85
    Rev. William, 85
Benjamin, Asher, 30, 32
Berger's House, 98
Blacksmiths, 26, 34, 37, 202
Bramah, John, 177
Brick, 32, 74, 93-94, 98, 100-04, 111, 129, 153, 155, 211
    bonding, 100
    cleaning of, 101
    corbelling, 159
    Flemish bond, 101
    -infill, 82, 85, 162, 168
    kilns, 95, 98, 129
    -layers, 98-99
    salmon, 100
    spalling, 102
Butternut, 90
By, Colonel, 100

Caldwell, Alexander, 88
Canadian Corps of Engineers, 85
Canadian Underwriters Association, 68
Cape Breton, 129

Carlow Lodge, 157
Carpenters, 27, 198
Ceilings, 163, 174-75, 182, 191-92
    tin, 67
Cellars, 81, 160
Chair-rails, 44, 201
Checkley, Colonel, 188
China, 190, 212
Chinking, 110-11
Cisterns, 75, 136, 138
Cladding, 85, 89-90, 122, 129-30, 132, 140. *See also*
    Siding, Roofs
    board and batten, 86, 90
    clapboard, 58, 85, 88-90, 129
    shingle, 85, 87, 90, 129, 132-34, 136
    tile, 129, 131, 136
Classical, 140, 191
    Revival, 94
Colombage pierrotte, 85
Condensation, 75, 80 81, 132, 137, 149, 160, 163, 168
Connecticut, 191
    Norwich, 199
Copings, 93
Cornices, 44, 104, 135-36, 193-94. *See also* Eaves
Crawl spaces, 80-81, 111, 155, 163
Creosote, 160
Crysler House, 31
Cupboards, 44-45
    built-in, 45, 48
    corner, 59
    lined, 90
    pie, 44

Delaware, 93
    Bay, 104
Dining rooms, 42
Don Valley Pressed Brick Works Catalogue, 99
Doors, 60-61, 105, 111, 116, 125-28, 163, 182, 198, 200,
    202, 205
    Cross and Bible, 125, 127
    double-panel, 127
    Federalist, 127-28
    four-panel, 128
    frames for, 85, 105
    hardware for, 125, 203

linings of, 90
Loyalist, 125-26
panel, 125-26
plank, 125, 127, 206
sills of, 90, 125-26
six-panel, 64
Dormers, 93, 137, 140
Dovetails, 111
Downing, A.J., 12, 140, 212
Downspouts, 130
Drainage, 77, 82, 94, 130, 137, 143
Dressers, 44-45
Drywall, 163, 171, 194
Dutch, 93, 101, 116, 129

Eaton, Moses, 191
Eaves, 135-37. *See also* Cornices
    boxed in, 136
Eavestroughing, 75, 77-78, 138
Edwardian, 12, 157, 179, 196, 210
Efflorescence, 102
Electricians, 81, 173-74
Elizabethan, 177
Elm, 90
Encyclopedia of Cottage, Farm and Villa Architecture, 140
England, 26, 94, 116, 129, 172, 190

Facades, 32, 98, 116
Fan lights, 121
Fay & Co., J.A., 199
Fences, 212-13
Fenestration, 116, 132
Finkle, Henry, 85
Fireplaces, 37, 45, 149, 151-53, 157-60, 162-63, 198
    chimneys, 93, 136, 139, 151, 157, 160, 162
    hearthstones, 160
    mantels, 160
    taxes on, 153
Fleeson, Plunkett, 190
Floors, 18, 61, 74, 78, 80-81, 90, 105, 111, 157, 160, 182, 191, 195, 198
    bridging, 81, 85
    cloths for, 191
    jacking, 81
    sanding, 74

stenciling, 191
support systems, 80-82
Forge du St. Maurice, 149, 153
Foundations, 60, 74-75, 77-79, 82, 93, 97, 105, 137, 140, 160, 162
Framing, 85-88
    balloon, 83, 85, 88
    braced, 88
    timber, 61, 82-83, 85, 88, 93, 116, 153
France, 26, 34, 190
Franklin, Benjamin, 149, 152
French Robertson House, 136, 138
Freeze-thaw cycle, 74, 77, 102, 129, 132, 136, 155
Furniture, 42, 44, 49, 69, 90, 191, 195, 205
The Furniture of French Canada, 93
Furniture of the Pilgrim Century, 182

Gables, 14, 20, 67, 137, 139, 140
Garrets, 132. *See also* Attics
Georgian, 30-32, 61, 68, 140, 190
    Frontier, 104
Germany, 93, 149
Gillies, John, 88
Gilz-Well Auger Company, 178
Glass, 116, 120-22, 124, 124-25, 163
    art (stained), 120
    cames, 116
    Crown, 116, 124
    lights, 116, 121
    making of, 116, 120
    panes, 120, 122
    plates, 120
    quarries, 116
Goad Company, Charles E., 68
Gourlay, Robert, 94
Greek, 198
    Revival, 32, 140
Gutters, 80, 102, 130, 132, 140
    copper, 138
    interior, 136-37

Hardware, 37, 61, 64, 125, 202-03
    fireplace, 162
    hinges, 202, 206
    latches, 37, 203

locks, 64, 202
   machine-made, 88
Harrington, Sir John, 177
Heating, 44, 58, 93, 148-68, 207
   baseboard, 153-54
   conduction, 154, 163
   contractors, 81
   convection, 154, 163
   ductwork, 150, 155-57
   forced air, 153, 155, 157, 163
   fuels for, 149, 153, 157
   furnaces, 80, 153
   radiation, 154, 160, 162-63
   radiators for, 155, 157, 160
   solar, 162, 165-67
   transfer holes, 151
Heron's Mills, 88
Holland, 98
Hudson Valley, 93, 98
Humidifiers, 157, 160

Industrial Revolution, 34, 36-37, 43, 99
Insecticides, 74, 91
Insulation, 111, 132, 148, 162-68, 170-71, 211
   R values, 163
   types of, 163, 166
   vapor barriers for, 132, 155, 168, 171
Insurers' Advisory Organization, 68

James House, 40, 43
Jennings, George, 177
Joinery, 26, 85, 182, 196-202
Joists, 80-81, 85, 90, 111, 175
   undersized, 80-81, 85

Kalm, Peter, 149
Kitchens, 40, 42, 45, 48, 50-51, 61, 64, 93, 140, 149,
   151-52, 155, 168, 178, 198, 200, 206

Labroust, 34
Landscape, 58, 77, 116, 182, 207-08, 212-14
Langley, Batty, 30
Lath, 64, 90, 153, 166, 193-94. *See also* Plaster
   accordion, 64, 193
   machine-made, 64, 193
   panes, 194

Le Fave, Minor, 32
Le June, Father, 26
Lighting, 58
   types of, 172
Lime, 94
   –stone, 94
Lintels, 90
Log buildings, 28, 85, 93, 104-113, 174
Lord House, 197
Louden, J.C., 140
Lower Canada, 120
Loyalist, 31-32, 100, 125
Lumber
   drives, 27, 85, 88
   pit-sawn, 34, 61, 84, 88
   plain-sawn, 88
   sawmill, 34, 84

McIntyre, Samuel, 30
McMahon, Bernard, 212
Maine, 15, 43, 87, 131, 152, 189, 198
   Limerick, 127
   North Berwick, 127-28, 152, 199
   Searsport, 167
Mallory, Nathaniel, 120
Manitoba
   East Selkirk, 95
Maple, 149
Maritimes, 191
Maryland, 98
Masonry, 93-104
   masons, 27, 93-104, 162
Massachusetts, 30, 40
   Boston, 40
   Cambridge, 40
Mennonites, Swiss, 93
Minhinnick, Jean, 42, 184
The Modern Builder's Guide, 32
Moisture damage, 74-75, 90, 93, 96, 120, 126, 130
Moodie, J.W.D., 149
Morris, Robert, 30
Mortar, 74, 78, 94-98, 102, 111, 159-60
Mortise and tenon, 35, 91
Mouldings, 61, 105, 163, 182, 194, 196, 198-99, 202
Munsell Color Chart, 188
Murdock, William, 172

Nails, 132, 136, 153, 166, 202
  machine-made, 37, 64
  rose-headed, 34, 64, 117, 193, 206
Neoclassical, 14, 136, 184, 198, 205
New Amsterdam, 98
New Brunswick, 120
  King's Landing, 152, 184
  St. Andrews, 139
New England, 18, 61, 85, 88, 128, 142, 158, 160, 164-65,
  167, 171, 183, 193, 206
New Hampshire
  Keene, 199
New Jersey, 94
New York, 129, 177
  New Utrecht, 129
North Carolina, 149
Nova Scotia, 15, 118
  Annapolis, 93
  Port Royal, 26, 93
Nutting, Wallace, 182

Oak, 85, 90, 91, 129, 182
Old Reach, 98
Ontario, 20, 21, 30, 32, 40, 43, 56, 58, 68, 86, 93, 120, 126,
  130-31, 135, 137, 142-43, 153, 158, 164, 166, 191, 193
  Belleville, 98
  Burritt's Rapids, 61, 157
  Cobourg, 99
  Gilroy Settlement, 33
  Hamilton, 95
  Kingston, 85
  Lanark County, 21, 26, 32, 40, 88, 107
  Leeds County, 41
  Mallorytown, 120
  Merrickville, 141
  Niagara, 98: -on-the-Lake, 126; Peninsula, 61
  North Augusta, 188
  Ontario County, 98
  Perth, 94, 127
  Port Perry, 98
  Rideau Canal, 100; corridor, 92, 97, 100, 126
  Scugog Township, 98
  Toledo, 188
  Toronto, 15, 142
  Upper Canada Village, 22, 151, 168, 190

Ottawa River, 85
  Valley, 27, 84

Paint, 45, 64, 80, 85, 104, 120, 122, 124, 132, 140, 157,
  162-63, 182-93, 195-96, 199
  dating, 187
  exterior, 194
  factory-made, 184
  fancy, 190-91, 195
  hand-mixed, 182, 184
  marbelizing, 187, 190
  removers, 74, 188, 196-97
  sanding, 195-96
  scagliola, 190
  spatter, 191
  stenciling, 187, 191, 193
  stripping, 74, 104, 195-96
  woodgraining, 186, 187-90, 196, 205
Palardy, Jean, 93
Palladio, 30
Paneling, 67, 90, 182, 198
Parapets, 93
Parging, 80, 98
Parlors, 40, 42, 46, 149, 151, 158, 160, 191, 205
Pediments, 194, 198
Pennsylvania, 104
  Lancaster County, 93
Philadelphia, 190
Pine, 186, 190, 193, 196
Pittsburgh Glass Company, 120
Plaster, 60, 64, 67, 80, 82, 153, 155, 157, 160, 163, 182,
  187, 192-94, 201
  decorative, 193
  keys of, 193-94
Plumbers, 81
  plumbing, 80, 148, 174-75, 177-78, 207
Pointing, 74, 80, 82, 94, 96-97, 98, 102, 104
Poles, 116
Pontil iron, 120
Porches, 60, 93, 116, 140-45. *See also* Verandahs
Portland Cement, 96-97
Posts, corner, 90
  jack, 81-82, 85
Practical House Carpenter, 32
Preservation, 12, 23, 54, 57, 64, 68, 74, 85, 90, 98-99,
  104-05, 153, 160, 167, 182, 195, 198, 214

Preservatives, 80, 122, 124-25, 140, 145, 194

Quebec, 19, 26, 29-32, 85, 87, 93, 98, 120, 129-31, 198
  City, 97
  French Regime, 19, 26, 131, 203
  Ile Saint Croix, 26
  Melbourne, 129
  Trois Rivières, 149
Queen Anne, 26
Quoins, 102

Rafters, 75, 88, 111, 129-30, 132, 136
Reconstruction, 23
Rehabilitation, 14, 23, 47, 55-56, 116, 160, 172, 174
  adaptive, 23, 54
  historical, 14, 16-17, 23, 50, 54, 56-57, 148, 158, 206
Reproductions, 194, 199, 202
Restoration, 12, 14, 22-23, 45, 70, 116, 121, 136, 140, 179,
  187
  specialists in, 57, 70, 187, 202
Revolutionary War, 116
Richardson, Henry, 34. See also Romanesque
Robinson, Jonas, 41
Roger & Co., C.B., 199
Rolph House, 188
Roman Baths, 174, 177
  buildings, 198
Romanesque, American, 32
  Richardson, 34, 142
Roofs, 75, 77-79, 93, 97, 105, 110, 116, 129-37, 140, 160,
  163. See also Cladding
  asphalt, 129-30, 132
  crimped-seam, 131
  cross-hatched, 129
  flashing for, 91, 93, 130, 136, 139-40
  log, 129
  raised batten, 129, 131-132
  raised seam, 129
  sheathing for, 91, 130
  slate, 129, 131-32
  standing seam, 131
  thatched, 129
Rot, 82, 93, 140
  dry, 81, 120, 194
  wet, 81, 111, 120, 136, 140, 149, 168

Roughing It in the Bush, 149
Rumford, Count, 152, 159, 161-62

Saint John River Valley, 189
St. Lawrence River, 153
St. Louis, 178
Sandblasting, 103-04
Scandinavia, 104, 195
Scotland, 85, 94
  masons from, 97
  Scots, 26, 94
Sealants, 91
Second Empire, 15
Seepage, 75-80
Sheathing, 91, 110, 129, 134, 193
Shingles, 77. See also Cladding
  asphalt, 110
  cedar, 111
Siding, 90, 136. See also Cladding
  ashlar, 86, 93
  bevel, 90
  tongue-and-groove, 89, 90
Sills, 90
Skylights, 139-40
Space usage, 148, 172, 195, 206
Spalding, William, 94
Staircases, 105
Stokes, Peter John, 23
Stone, 32, 58-59, 74, 92-104, 111, 123, 153, 171
  ashlar, 94
  bond stones, 97
  cleaning, 102-04
  headers, 97
  rip-rap, 97
  rubble -, 12, 20, 21, 61, 78, 80, 91, 93-98, 103, 162, 166
Stoves, 42, 44, 67, 149, 151, 153-54, 158, 160, 165
  Franklin, 149, 152
  pipes for, 150, 157
  St. Maurice, 153
  Scottish, 153
Stucco, 94, 98
Studs (quarters), 88, 157, 163
Sump pump, 79-80

Thoroughgood House, 129
Tinsmith, 129, 138

Tools, 26, 34, 37, 85, 88, 193
Transoms, 120, 126
Travels in North America, 149
Trusses, 129-30
Tyndall stone, 95

Valances, 198
Ventilation, 80, 132, 149, 163, 168, 170, 175, 178, 184, 190, 195-96
Verandahs, 116, 140-45, 209. *See also* Porches
Vernacular style, 32
Victorian, 12, 15, 32, 37, 43, 66-67, 101, 119-20, 129, 136-37, 140, 157, 163, 176, 179, 200, 212
    Gothic, 34, 142
Virginia, 26, 85, 128-29, 198
    Jamestown, 98, 116
    Virginia Beach, 129
    Williamsburg, 98

Wainscot, 64, 182, 198
Wallpaper, 64, 80, 163, 186, 190
Walls, 75, 81, 85, 90, 96, 104-05, 109, 116, 123, 156-57, 162-63, 166
Walnut, 90
War of 1812, 85
Waste disposal, 177-79
Weeping tiles, 80, 178
Wells, 175, 179, 212
White Swan Hotel, 61
Windows, 42, 54, 58-59, 105, 108-09, 111, 116-25, 137, 163, 172, 182, 187, 195, 200
    aluminum, 163
    awnings for, 162
    Carpenter Gothic, 121
    casement, 116
    double-hung, 116, 163
    frames for, 90, 124
    glazing, 111, 116-17, 121
    munton bars, 116, 120
    nine-over-nine, 120
    oriel, 68
    oval, 122
    reproduction, 119
    sashes for, 117, 120-22
    shutters for, 120, 162, 166, 206
    sills for, 120, 122
    six-over-six, 121
    stone, 104
    storm, 121, 154, 162-63, 172
    thermopane, 172
    twelve-over-twelve, 117
Wiring, 148, 166, 168-69, 172-74, 178, 207
Woodwork, 154, 163, 171, 195, 198
Woodworth, William, 198
Wren, Sir Christopher, 27